brilliant

personal
development

PEARSON

At Pearson, we believe in learning – all kinds of learning for all kinds of people. Whether it's at home, in the classroom or in the workplace, learning is the key to improving our life chances.

That's why we're working with leading authors to bring you the latest thinking and the best practices, so you can get better at the things that are important to you. You can learn on the page or on the move, and with content that's always crafted to help you understand quickly and apply what you've learned.

If you want to upgrade your personal skills or accelerate your career, become a more effective leader or more powerful communicator, discover new opportunities or simply find more inspiration, we can help you make progress in your work and life.

Pearson is the world's leading learning company. Our portfolio includes the Financial Times, Penguin, Dorling Kindersley, and our educational business, Pearson International.

Every day our work helps learning flourish, and wherever learning flourishes, so do people.

To learn more please visit us at: www.pearson.com/uk

personal
development

Your essential guide to an all-round successful life

Max A. Eggert

Harlow, England • London • New York • Boston • San Francisco • Toronto • Sydney • Auckland • Singapore • Hong Kong
Tokyo • Seoul • Taipei • New Delhi • Cape Town • São Paulo • Mexico City • Madrid • Amsterdam • Munich • Paris • Milan

PEARSON EDUCATION LIMITED

Edinburgh Gate
Harlow CM20 2JE
Tel: +44 (0)1279 623623
Website: www.pearson.com/uk

First published 2013 (print and electronic)

Pearson Education is not responsible for the content of third party internet sites.

ISBN: 978-0-273-74247-0 (print)
       978-0-273-74248-7 (PDF)
       978-0-273-74249-4 (ePub)

British Library Cataloguing-in-Publication Data
A catalogue record for the print edition is available from the British Library

Library of Congress Cataloging-in-Publication Data
Eggert, Max.
   Brilliant personal development : your essential guide to an all-round successful life / Max Eggert. -- 1 Edition.
     pages cm
   Includes index.
   ISBN 978-0-273-74247-0 (pbk). -- ISBN (invalid) 978-1-273-74248-7 (pdf) -- ISBN (invalid) 978-0-273-74249-4 (ePub) 1. Success. 2. Self-actualization (Psychology) 3. Assertiveness (Psychology) 4. Self-esteem. I. Title.
   BF637.S8E344 2012
   650.1--dc23
                        2012039526

10 9 8 7 6 5 4 3 2 1
17 16 15 14 13

Print edition typeset in 10/14pt Plantin by 3
Printed in Great Britain by Henry Ling Ltd., at the Dorset Press, Dorchester, Dorset

NOTE THAT ANY PAGE CROSS REFERENCES REFER TO THE PRINT EDITION

This text is dedicated to Father Terrance Dix, Father John Moody, Father Jim Glennon (RIP), Father Glen Stewart (RIP) and Father Neil Macintosh, all at some time fellow priests in the Parish of St Mary the Virgin, Bondi, without whom my spiritual development would be indigent, what wisdom I have impoverished, and the ability to laugh at myself less feasible.

Contents

About the author

'Max is an international management psychologist who has the gift of making the complexities of human behaviour understandable and relevant to business.'

Financial Times

Max A. Eggert is Chief Psychologist with Transcareer, an International Management Psychology Consultancy. He has been interviewed frequently on TV, on radio and in the print media both in Europe and in Australia. His work and publications have been reviewed both in the professional journals and in the specialist media. He has also lectured at premier universities as well as leading many professional conferences.

Max first read theology as a preparation for his ordination for the priesthood and through his fascination with people undertook degrees in psychology and industrial relations, and postgraduate studies in clinical hypnosis. Several of his books are on the recommended reading lists of London, Sydney, Harvard, Westminster and Sussex Universities.

Married to Jane, with four children between them, Max lives in Bondi Beach Australia and, as an Anglo-Catholic priest, his joy and privilege is as one of the Pavement Priests working on the streets within the Archdiocese of Sydney for those in need of prayer and a sympathetic ear. He also leads the Community of Our Lady of Advent, one of several Anglican worshiping communities in Sydney. When not praying, writing, consulting or counselling, his other consuming passions are riding his thoroughbred, Zeus, walking his dogs, Daisy and Bana, failing to prevent the three cats, Solomon, Sheba and Pierre, from destroying china mementoes and praying that Mary, his Eclectus parrot, will not use the 'F' expletive when there are dinner parties.

Max can be contacted at Max@transcareer.com.au or at fr.max@communitiesofourlady.asn.com and you can discover more about his secular work at **www.transcareer.com.au**

Acknowledgements

The Transcareer Team

Taking time off and giving myself early marks three days a week to write this text meant that many colleagues and friends had to take up my not inconsiderable workload whilst I indulged myself in undertaking this interesting project – thanks, guys.

Clients

Since working in Australia I have enjoyed the support and assistance of numerous clients because as a Management Psychologist, clients always guarantee that you are climbing a very steep learning curve to ensure that your pragmatic recommendations, derived from a soft academic base, are right first time – thanks, guys.

The real workers

Writing gives you a much larger shadow than you deserve and I thank my wife, soul mate, best friend and adviser, Jane, for all the indulgences she has given me. To Victoria and Anthony, my beautiful step-children, for their support in the Chardonnay department. Finally to my dogs, Bana and Daisy, for keeping my three cats, Solomon, Sheba and Pierre, out of the study and their paws off my keyboard when I took breaks – thanks, guys.

Editorial support

As one who is a great starter but poor finisher I most certainly would have struggled with this project if it had not been for the continual support of the Pearson editorial team. Accolades and gratitude must go to Samantha Jackson, my Acquisitions Editor, who was more than adequately supported by Elie Williams, Laura Blake, Senior Editor, and especially Rachel Hayter, Editorial Assistant, who through her frequent demands for progress reports ensured I attempted to make my target of 1500 words on my writing days – thanks, guys.

R&R

Writing not only takes research but also reflection and thinking time, and so I was blessed that within a three-minute stroll I could undertake this important right-brain activity on the beautiful Bondi Beach. Prince Charles may talk to flowers; my solace is talking to the waves of the Tasman Sea that twice a day roll up the beach just to check up on progress or for a discussion on a particular point – thanks, waves.

Publisher's acknowledgements

The 75 body-language signs table on pages 284–8 courtesy of Gabrielle Griffin.

Before you begin

The Marshmallow Tests

Between 1968 and 1974 Walter Mischel ran some interesting tests on children, which were to become famously known as the 'Marshmallow Tests'.

Mischel took a group of 337 girls and 316 boys who had just turned four. Once they felt relaxed in the presence of a psychologist they were seated at a table which had three items on it: a small bell, one marshmallow on its own, and two marshmallows together.

The psychologist explained that the adults were about to leave the room and that the child had a choice to make: if they could wait until the psychologist returned then they could have the reward of two marshmallows, but if the child did not want to wait they could ring the bell which would bring an adult into the room and they could have the single marshmallow immediately.

As you've probably realised this was an experiment measuring delayed gratification – bread today for jam, or in this case marshmallows, tomorrow. How long could a child hold out before succumbing to the temptation of a single marshmallow?

The results of the initial tests showed how well the children were at controlling their primitive brain – the immediate fight-or-flight part of the brain (limbic system) which whispered, and in some cases shouted, 'eat now' – and whether they could shift into using their modern thinking brain (cortex) and develop the equation:

$$Sc = R \times 2$$

Where Sc = Self-control and R = Reward.

The average time the children managed before ringing the bell was nine minutes. But some, obviously very high on self-control, managed an incredible 20 minutes.

So this is an interesting experiment on self-control, but why is it here at the beginning of a book on self-development? Because of what happened next.

Mischel revisited the children in adolescence. Those demonstrating greater self-control as four year olds had in later life developed the following positive character traits:

- greater fluency in their speech
- greater attention span
- better concentration
- greater stress resilience
- more self-assurance
- more honesty (i.e. less likely to cheat at anything)
- watched less TV in favour of homework
- did better in exams
- were not overweight.

Now this is where it gets really, really interesting.

At age 27 those adults who as children just could not wait to enjoy the marshmallow, the under four-minute children, were more likely to:

- have fewer formal qualifications

- have difficulties relating to others
- have an alcohol or drug problem
- have a police record
- have a poor employment record
- be aggressive
- be overweight or obese.

What Mischel had proved almost conclusively was that self-control, or in the psychological jargon, 'executive functioning for delayed gratification', is a far better prediction of both academic and 'life success'. That is why this research on the psychology of self-control fronts this text.

In self-development we are in it for the long haul. To do this, and to keep going, we need to pass the Marshmallow Test and manage our self-control. If you are serious about developing yourself then you are in the business of delayed gratification: bread today for jam tomorrow; effort today for benefits tomorrow. So it doesn't matter how old you are or how clever you are, without self-control your self-development will be impoverished.

And if you ever waver, remember that the moment self-control fails us on an ongoing basis, and we forget the advantages and benefits of personal change, we will fall back into being who we were. Then, when those feelings of needing to improve return, as they always do, we become disappointed with our previous lack of personal control and self-discipline. Such self-thoughts are definitely not healthy.

Please keep in mind that the strong desire to improve is the rocket fuel of achievement and that self-discipline will be the gyroscope that keeps us on the straight and narrow path. It is not all graft, though, since gratification will be in the effort as well as the reward.

So let's begin our journey of self-development with the sage words of the novelist George Eliot:

'It is never too late to be what you might have been.'

The way this text works

As you will have seen from the contents list, this text brings together the most pressing areas in self-development in one volume. I doubt very much that when you flicked through it you thought you would need to brush up on every topic, so the text has been designed with complete sections for you to dip into depending on your particular interest. However, I hope that in your dipping you might be encouraged to swim into other chapters.

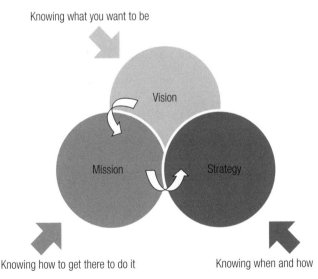

Please appreciate that in such an important area as self-development the writer also writes for himself, constantly reminding himself that he is still on the journey and, as my congregation, university students and family continually remind me, I have a fair way to go yet. This being the case, sometimes I give myself the liberty of self-disclosure when I feel it illustrates a valid point or is a reasonable example to put some flesh on the theory. Also, being on the journey myself, I lapse occasionally into the first-person singular, so I hope this causes more amusement than offence.

Each chapter usually has some activities. Doing is always more powerful than just reading. Can I urge you to undertake and reflect on the activities? In this way the text will become more personal and, because you are undertaking the activities, more effective. Up until 1476 most people had no choice but to learn by oral tradition and doing. Learning through activity, especially personal development, is still the most effective and enduring method. May I ask those of you who buy high-tech gadgets and start pressing buttons without first reading the manual (you, by the way, enjoy a 'pragmatic' style of learning) to read the chapter first (in spite of the caveat above) and then undertake the activities. Activity without a cognitive structure brings little development value, just as a building without a structure soon collapses.

I have a penchant for quotations. I find that even if I cannot remember all the substance of a topic, a remembered quote can spark the significant points that assist recall. However, just as 'A stitch in time saves nine' and 'More haste less speed' are contradictory, they still contain wisdom. There will be quotations that appear incongruous until you put them in context. After many years working as a psychologist and as a priest it is my experience that we, too, are a paradox of contradictions. These you may discover as you enter into the spirit of some of the activities in the text.

I don't wish you luck in your personal development because luck, as shown in the Marshmallow Tests, has little to do with personal development. I just wish you every success in becoming the person you wish to be and maximising the full potential of all your talents.

Remember, in the last analysis, it only takes one person to develop your life – you!

Father Max A. Eggert OPC
Community Priest, The Communities of Our Lady, Sydney,
Australia

Introduction: first things first

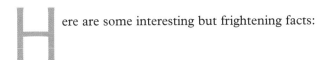ere are some interesting but frightening facts:

- Most people work harder for their employer than they do for themselves.
- Most people spend more time planning their next holiday than they do planning their lives.
- Most people spend more money on hygiene and beauty products in a year than they do on their own development in a lifetime.
- Most people spend more time watching television in a month than they do thinking about their career in their entire lives.

This book is not for them.

Let me start with some home truths. Let's deal with the scary ones first and then get on to the real advantages:

- **Personal development is about being honest with yourself.** We structure our own lives and shape our individuality. The decisions we make are ours, consequently we must be honest and recognise that we are responsible for who we are.
- **Personal development is hard work.** If it weren't, there would be many more successful people in the world.

- **Personal development has no short cuts**. If there were then there would again be many more successful people in the world.

- **Personal development costs friendships**. Everyone wants you to be successful but not more successful than they are.

- **Personal development involves risk**. Niccolò Machiavelli once wrote 'Never was anything great achieved without danger', and personal development is all about achievement.

And now for the goodies:

- **Personal development brings great happiness**. Since you are completely at home with yourself.

- **Personal development brings fantastic ego strength**. Since you can rightly claim that you did it your way.

- **Personal development brings you wealth in whatever form you conceive it to be**. Since you will not stay in a boring job, put up with boring people or spend time doing boring things or with people you don't respect.

- **Personal development brings you health, both in body and in mind**. In pursuing your future, your body will go with you so you'll naturally look after it.

- **Personal development will make you attractive**. Everyone is drawn to successful people in whatever life they choose to pursue.

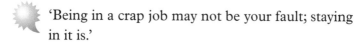 'Being in a crap job may not be your fault; staying in it is.'

Sally Hogshead, consultant and author

Now, are you ready for brilliant personal development?

Eight signs you might need to work on yourself

1. You are not achieving to your best ability in many areas of your life

We all go through slumps, bad days, even bad weeks when we just do not give our best … but what if those weeks turn into months? If there is no challenge in what you do then you are in danger of 'rust out' which is the opposite of 'burnout'.

2. You start gravitating towards people with whom you can be disgruntled

Think about the people with whom you choose to socialise both in your leisure and at work. Who do you seek out? Are you drawn toward the malcontents, the people who derive pleasure from complaining? How true it is that: 'He who lies down with dogs, shall rise up with fleas.'

3. You begin to feel that your future is grey and on a holding pattern

Does your life look much the same in the future as it is now? Are you repeating the same old patterns of behaviour? If your life is perfect and you are content then that's fine. But I'm guessing that you wouldn't be reading this text if life were perfect. If you want to make improvements to your life you need to challenge yourself to be someplace else at some point in the near future.

4. You take inventory of your situation's pros and cons … and the cons win

If you're having a hard time deciding whether to move forward or you find yourself just treading water in the river of life, try this very simple exercise:

Create a document with two lists: things you like about your current situation – lifestyle, relationships, job, etc. (the pros), and things you dislike (the cons). If the cons outweigh the pros on a particular aspect of your life then now is the time to do something about it. So often for people in this situation others start to make decisions for them: your partner asks for a divorce or your manager fires you or makes you redundant.

5. You look for ways to improve your current situation but you have no room to manoeuvre towards your aspirations

Another useful activity is to take your list of pros from the previous activity and expand upon it. Elaborate on the items already on the list and add other items you wish you could claim about your current situation. When you've finished, since you cannot change everything, just review the list for items you may be able to improve upon or make happen in your present situation. The Americans have a wonderful saying for this: 'By the inch it is a cinch but by the yard it is very hard.'

So keep working on the inches and keep the big picture in mind. If this sounds too simplistic take a hint from Martina Navratilova, six times Wimbledon champion, who when asked how she dealt with all the pressure on centre court, replied:

'I don't worry about winning the point, the game, the set or the championship. I just have to hit the ball over the net.'

6. You can't get enough positive reinforcement to keep your spirits up

Feeling valued is one of the cornerstones of your sense of wellbeing. It's one of those things money can't buy. We all vary in terms of our need to feel valued and it's important you become aware of your own needs and then develop techniques for meeting those needs. Keeping a log is valuable here as is a list of all your achievements both in life and in work. Review your log frequently when you need encouragement and remind yourself of how much you have done.

Personal rewards are useful here, too, and as they are so important we will deal with them more fully later.

7. Your life or work situation has changed radically in the past 12 months

Your life used to be pretty good, but now it has lost its thrill and challenge. If such a change occurs, there are three choices: do something about it; go with the flow and make the most of the situation (not advised); or complain to anyone who might listen (not advised).

8. You are a born worrier

Statisticians at the University of Wisconsin have studied the things that we worry about. They found that the average individual's worries can be divided into four headings:

- 40% – things that never happened
- 30% – things that happened that the individual can't change
- 22% – petty worries of insignificance
- 8% – legitimate worries

'Worry is wasting today's time to clutter up tomorrow's opportunities with yesterday's trouble.'

Let's clear the clutter.

'There is one prerequisite for managing the next part of your life:
You must begin doing so before you enter it.'

Peter Drucker, management guru

CHAPTER 1

The makings of brilliant personal development

B efore we start our journey of self-development there are some 'makings' that we have to undertake if we are to be successful, and there are six of them:

1. Making commitments to yourself

First of all an apology: this text, and, by the way, thank you for investing in it, will not change you. Other people will not change you. Only you can change you. Others can guide, advise, train, mentor, motivate and coach; they can even hound, nag, badger, pester and threaten, but in the end it has to be you.

There is a very simple little mantra, which we repeat several times in the text, which goes:

'If it's going to be, then it's down to me.'

You are, for the most part, in control of your life and this is particularly so in how you wish to develop yourself, the skills you want to enjoy and the person you wish to become.

Most of my clients, until we work together, labour far harder for their employer and their managers than they do for themselves. They know far more about their organisation, its mission and values and what it hopes to achieve than the very same aspects of themselves. It's as if we leave planning and making a full life for ourselves and our families at home when we go to work and are too tired to do anything about it when we come home. Our own development is like the elephant in the room: we know it's there and we should be doing something, but somehow we manage to ignore it and not even budge a trunk of it.

Fortunately, or unfortunately, life is not a dress rehearsal; there is only one shot and no action replay. However, we don't need a replay to learn from our errors and mistakes.

T.S. Eliot, the poet, in a rare moment of simplicity wrote:

'We had the experience but missed the meaning.'

Each day is full of potential for development, with lessons and development milestones achieved with willing coaches and mentors. But only if we commit to it.

Two million years ago something wonderful occurred – the size of our ancestors' brains, at breakneck speed for evolution, doubled in size and our sloping brows transformed into foreheads to cope with this phenomenon. More importantly, in moving from *Homo habilis* to *Homo sapiens* we were gifted with frontal lobes which endowed us with the facility to think and plan ahead, to dream dreams of what could be, rather than just having the stimulus and response of what is. We now enter the world with the capacity for constructing wonderful imaginings of what we 'want to be' and enjoy all the enthusiasm that attends personal challenge.

I hope I am not a huge finger-wagger, but it amazes me that literally millions of people spend hours in the gym and/or thousands of pounds on make-up yet no time at all on their minds or their personal development. Such action is certainly good for the body but it's rather like polishing your car in the hope of avoiding a service or hoping it will make the engine more efficient so it lasts longer.

Life is short and, without self-care and self-commitment, all too suddenly, 30 years later, the self-talk of 'I am going to be' takes a nosedive and is diluted to 'I could have been'. Whilst this may sound depressing, the fact is it is never too late to start again. Even if you have lost most of the battles, the war is never over if you decide to marshal your resources once more.

 'Failure is not about falling down but making the conscious decision not to get up again.'

Anon.

Investing in a text such as this in terms of money and the opportunity costs of reading it demands a degree of commitment. Whilst psychologists never give guarantees, when you make a commitment to yourself that you want to develop the muscles of your inner self, there will always be an equitable dividend.

 'Getting ahead in a difficult profession requires avid faith in yourself. That is why some people with mediocre talent, but with great inner drive, go so much further than people with vastly superior talent.'

Sophia Loren, actress

 'More people fail through lack of purpose than through lack of talent.'

Billy Sunday, American athlete

2. Making the results worth it

A friend was desperate to have a car of a certain type – up went the picture on the fridge; a man wanted to be more spiritually aware – so up went the picture of the Dalai Lama; a woman wanted to slim by two sizes so …

At a very basic level we are driven by pleasure or pain. Some postpone going to the dentist until the pain outweighs the fear. Not that there isn't any pain in self-development in terms of effort and investment, but it is nothing like toothache. There is more satisfaction and fun to be had when we can anticipate pleasurable and valuable outcomes in personal development. Your decision to invest time, money and effort is driven by the advantages that will accrue. Nobody goes to a gym because it has this or that exercise machine. They go to fulfil a desire – being fitter, being stronger, having bigger muscles or even to satisfy some social need such as meeting people and getting out of the house.

So the anticipated advantages keep us motivated and whisper continually in one ear 'do not give up' and in the other 'keep going'.

For the most part, the effort and time we spend in self-development, when put on the scales, comes down on the pleasure side, providing we keep the potential results in mind. However, if it was that easy, everyone would be into self-development in a big way.

Unfortunately, sometimes the pleasures of today – the single marshmallow – are more tempting than the pleasures of tomorrow. A marshmallow in the mouth now is worth two left on the table if I have to wait!

Making the most of you takes time, real effort and usually some financial investment. Unless there is commitment to the journey there is a good chance of slippage, then resignation, then into life's boxing ring flies the white towel. As we take this return trip back to the way we were, we are greeted by our dark friends 'guilt' and 'regret' and the accompanying thoughts, ' If only I had …' or, even worse, 'I should have but now I can't'.

The challenge

Up until this moment we have spent the whole of our lives behaving in the way that we have always done, so making significant changes in our thinking, our attitudes and our behaviour comes at a real cost in terms of effort and time. The way we are now is seemingly secure, so to embrace a different future will certainly test our resolve.

Experts tell us that it takes about 130 hours behind the wheel before we become reasonably efficient at driving a car. If it takes that long to learn to drive then to change from who we are to who we want to be will certainly take longer. In self-development we are in it for the long haul. To do this, and to keep going, we always need to keep the benefits in the forefront of our minds. The 'why', which is about benefits, helps the 'doing'. To be successful in our endeavours to grow and develop we need continually to remind ourselves of where we will be and what we will be able to do.

The moment we forget the advantages and benefits of personal change is the moment of slippage when we fall back to being who we were. Then, when we feel the need to change again, we become disappointed with our lack of determination.

Right now, unless you develop yourself you are all you are ever going to be. Once you begin to change you will never be what you were, but a new person with new skills and abilities. Too often we settle for too little and achieve it rather than stretching ourselves to discover the boundaries of our abilities. One of the best things about achievements that we accomplish in life is that no one can ever take them away from us.

It's rather like going to the gym or distance running when you have an endorphin hit: self-development bequeaths a confidence hit with your successes lasting forever.

As with running, the more you run the further you can go next time. It will be the same for you; your development 'muscles' will become stronger every time you flex them.

 **tip**

You owe it to your future to begin to get ready now.

 'Being OK, average or adequate is a given and only buys you a ticket to the game.'

Sally Hogshead

3. Making the process work

It is trite but right that 'nothing happens until you do something'. Self-development is about doing stuff and doing it regularly.

Most people could run a marathon but they could not do it tomorrow. They would have to follow a proper, sensible and regular training regime to be able to cover the 26 miles 385 yards.

One can have the grandest of designs but it will remain on the drawing board without action. As Confucius rightly said, and he said a lot of good things:

'Talk cannot grow rice.'

Good vision, good design, good process and good work will deliver good results.

Two stories from life
The General and the Brigadier
At one time I had the privilege of working with senior officers when they came out of the Services. Once I coached two officers, one a brigadier and the other a general. My session always began with the same statement: 'You have done well to have achieved a very successful Service career.' Back came the response from the brigadier: 'Yes I have, but if I had been as fortunate as Sir Peter over there I would have made general.'

When welcoming Sir Peter with the same question, he came back with the reply: 'Yes, when I was a junior subaltern I knew that to get a promotion I had to see some action in a conflict zone so what I did was … having achieved major I knew that I had to get my BTA (Been To America) so I wangled a job flying a desk for NATO in Washington, then went on to do diplomatic work in a variety of countries. As a brigadier, if I was to make general, I knew that I had to see some active service again so I engineered a posting to … and that is how I did so well and became a general. My personal battle plan worked.'

Making an assessment as a psychologist, I am sure that there was very little difference in the ability, motivation or intelligence of these two gifted Army officers. Sir Peter had the edge because he had a vision, developed a mission and kept to the plan. He stayed in the process, always identifying his next step, and worked the plan.

This might all sound mechanistic and a somewhat dry process-orientated approach. However, you are the person in charge of your vision, mission and plan, which you can change whenever you want.

The guitarist

A friend in his late teens was a brilliant guitarist, winning a place at the Royal School of Music. His vision was to be a concert guitarist. One summer he took a holiday in Spain and ended up in the beautiful fishing village of Peniscola on the Costa del Azahar, along the Mediterranean coast. He fell in love with the people, the town, the lifestyle and, of course, the music. His mission changed almost overnight and he is now a brilliant jondo flamenco guitarist who, with his singer, entertains aficionados from Valencia to Cartagena and beyond. One's mission, like one's mind, should never be set in concrete.

brilliant question and answer

Q How do you make God laugh?

A Tell him your plans!

brilliant tip

Before you make a significant step in life ask yourself: 'Where is this leading and what options does it give me?'

4. Making the investment

It's a startling fact that most of us will spend more time planning a holiday than planning the next stage of our lives. A great holiday is enjoyed and then it is back to the same old, same old. Relief from the day-to-day stuff comes from planning the next holiday. As we have already noted, most people will spend more money in a year on hygiene and beauty products than they will on their self-development during their lifetime. The roads are full of beautifully efficient cars being driven by less efficient people.

Once you become aware of this you can see that a bit more time spent thinking and planning for your future is a wise investment. And I'm not asking you to spend whole weekends or even an evening a week. Once you have done the preliminary work just 30 minutes a month is more than enough time to review what you have achieved over the month and you can list down what you want to do and achieve for the next month as well.

 'If you don't have a plan then you plan to fail!'

One of my organisational clients ran a rigorous training programme for its staff. Each employee worked with their manager to agree their development each year and a budget was allocated in terms of both time and cost. This worked well for the employees, who received the extra skills they needed, and the company, who dispensed with the need for long-winded approval processes because they knew from the start of the year what resources had been allocated.

Such an approach might also work for you. How much are you prepared to spend each year on your own personal development? Most people spend nothing, hoping the government or their employer will pick up the tab. Of course the employer may pick up the tab, but it will only be for what they want you to do. But what you want to do may be on a tangent or in a totally different direction, which is of no interest to your employer or any government scheme. Here it is again:

'If it's going to be, then it's down to me.'

5. Making 'me' time

This comes from my mother. We all loved fussing over her on Mother's Day as she justifiably basked indolently in her well-deserved attention. One day she announced that since Mother's Day came but once a year, from now on she was going to have regular 'me days'; that is a Mother's Day once a month. Her luxury was well-warranted. In a way we came to think of it as legitimate selfishness. Perhaps she took time off because she knew her Ovid:

'Take rest; a field that has rested gives a bountiful crop.'

In spiritual and religious circles the benefits of this have been known for thousands of years through the concept of taking a 'retreat'. Every now and again the religious take themselves off, out of their day-to-day world, just to pray, think and reflect.

For personal development we all need 'me time' to ensure that we are on the right track and staying on the rails by doing the right things. We owe it to ourselves to look after ourselves and rest is essential. As for my mother, she achieved and deserved her 'me time' once a month and was a better mum for it.

'Nobody gets to live life backward. Look ahead – that is where your future lies.'

Ann Landers, advice columnist (amending Kierkegaard)

6. Making focus

Focus acts like a scent and colour to a honey bee. You can't help being drawn to your goal and the closer you get, the more powerfully you are pulled towards your desired achievement.

It is a tautology but it's true that 'you see what you look for'. When you are hungry, having been for a long drive, what do you see in the next town? Restaurants of course! Once committed to your vision you cannot help but see opportunities that life presents.

We have much to learn from a strange fish called *Anableps anableps*. It is fantastically well adapted for survival. The pupil in each eye is horizontally divided into two parts, allowing it to see clearly below and above the water. This adaptation allows this fish to find food at or below the surface and also gives it extra protection against predators. Since it spends virtually all of its life swimming at the surface, it needs this extra protection. Take a look at this at **www.youtube.com/watch?v=mgOiIvFcN5I**.

We also must use our eyes in the same way: one looking at your present situation and the other looking always to the future to see what's on the horizon. Then you need to construct the best compromise between the two. A good soccer player plays in the

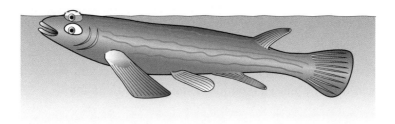

The Anableps anableps

'now' but can also read the game. He plays the ball whilst being conscious of the potential opportunities. To extend the analogy, it's keeping your eye on the ball of opportunities occurring in the game of life both current and long term.

Focus is the superglue that ensures your aspirations are firmly fixed. A mission without focus is like a ship without a crew – it just stays anchored in port. Focus is like a fox in the chicken coop – it just can't be ignored without losing all your chickens. (We work more on focus and its relationship to effort and energy later.)

Your written mission and focus enjoy a symbiotic relation-ship since they continually feed off each other as both become stronger.

As you have already discovered, there are so many demands on your time and your life. Personal, family, interests, work and the community all come at you like arrows from a thousand bows making their piercing demands as if you were Saint Sebastian. So, without focus on what is most important, the danger is that you will end up an 'I wisher': 'I wish I had done that', 'I wish I had spent time …', etc. Well that changes here and now. Now you are a doer, who can look back with pride on what you have achieved.

 **tip**

Grandma's law

When you have a list of things to achieve, a useful way to allocate your focus is to apply 'Grandma's law'. If your Gran was like mine then you will be familiar with: 'If you eat your vegetables then you can have your ice-cream.'

In other words, when you have your list of priorities for the day, week or month, list them with the worst first and then rank in order so whatever is most enjoyable comes last. If you reverse your list in terms of what you enjoy then each time you complete something the next gives greater pleasure.

7. Making it work

Working on yourself means following this process to get the most from this text:

● Dip into the sections of the text that appeal and study the parts that you find interesting.

● Reinforce the new ideas by undertaking the activities.

● Reflect on what you have done.

● Make a decision about what will work for you, passing over that which does not appeal.

● Set 'SMARTI' goals for yourself (we repeat this several times because it is so important):

  – **S**pecific

  – **M**easurable

  – **A**ctionable

  – **R**easonable – is it challenging and stretching, but not impossible?

- **Time-bound** – when will you finish?
- **Interesting** – is it a goal that appeals and challenges you?

● Experiment and practise new behaviour after the activities.

● Reflect on the results and the outcomes of the activities.

● Practise, practise, practise again.

● Recognise slippage and get back on track.

● Reward your progress (more on this later).

● Move onto your next SMARTI challenge.

 '**Tomorrow's battle is won during today's practice.**'

Japanese proverb

To be successful without taking action is like hoping to catch a fish without bait. Action is about movement: you could be on the right track but if you are not moving nothing will happen.

One of the reasons that McDonald's is successful is because when a new site is in the process of being selected it's all about location, location, location. To get to where you want to go after some practice it's action, action, action. Success is a troika of goal, focus and action; they are the holy trinity of personal development.

 '**When all is said and done, more is usually said than done.**'

Anon

 '**You cannot build a reputation on what you are going to do.**'

Henry Ford, car manufacturer

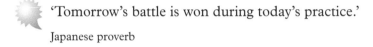 '**Just do it.**'

Nike slogan

With behaviour, nothing happens overnight; it takes time and lots of it. Just like flowers and trees, we are only as good as our root system. When we lack our 'action roots' then our development, if any, is severely stunted. If you find yourself becoming impatient consider the bamboo plant. This perennial evergreen can grow anything up to two feet in a day, but that baby bamboo spent seven years below ground before smashing through the surface to become the Olympian of the plant world that it is.

CHAPTER 2

Two things you might need … and a warning

B efore we set off there are two more things which will help you on the journey.

A log book

Within the inner fold of the temporal lobe there is a very old part of the cortex called the hippocampus, which manages your long-term memory. Once something is in your long-term memory you will have access to it throughout your life.

The trick is finding a way to transfer your learning from your short-term to your long-term memory. Keeping a log book is very effective in this respect since the very act of writing something down reinforces it in your memory. Use it to record time/dates, thoughts, reflections, learning points, choices, decisions, goals, strategies for actions, actions taken, failures, learning points and results. More importantly, use your log book to record your successes, your achievements and the steps you have completed. This will become an invaluable tool to keep your motivation high. Then, when you come across one of those slump days, you can look back and remember how far you have come and feel inspired to keep going.

 'The palest ink is better than the best memory.'

Confucius

Making time

Personal development takes time and effort and, as we have said before, most people treat their growth as the elephant in the room – they know that it's very important but somehow it's ignored. Life always demands that you deal with the ants (the small things) rather than the elephant. Of course dealing with the ants gives you a better headcount but the recompense is, in the long term, very disappointing. So, as part of your time management, make sure you book time out for your personal development activities. In addition, a little and often is better than huge and infrequent. Little and often soon becomes part of your lifestyle and will not feel like an obligation. Working on yourself for yourself should be enjoyable, fun and rewarding.

A fellow traveller

Deaf and blind from 19 months, Helen Keller became a global phenomenon. Not only was she a symbol of determination, discipline and courage, she was an extraordinary lesson in what can be achieved against all the odds. She was the first person with her limiting condition to gain an arts degree, but more than that she went on to become an author, political activist and lecturer, who devoted her life to helping others. If ever you feel that life has dealt you a bad hand read her story and get things into proportion.

As well as being a remarkable woman, Helen had the distinct advantage of having someone who wholeheartedly supported her. This was her inspirational tutor, Anne Sullivan. It was because of Anne's unfailing belief in her that Helen reached the heights she did.

On your own journey of self-development you may find it useful to find a friend who would like to take the journey with you. You'll find it more fun, more enlightening and more enduring with a companion.

'Walking with a friend in the dark is better than walking alone in the light.'

Helen Keller, author and activist

brilliant activity

- Set regular times for development activity.
- Use a log book for your goals, activities, actions and successes.
- Work with a friend.

And remember PPO: Persistence Pays Off.

A warning: The reasons why people fail

1 They do not have a vision, a mission or a direction for themselves.

2 They do not put in the effort or time to improve themselves.

3 They lack ambition and are content with being average.

4 They spend no time looking for opportunities.

5 They find it difficult to take risks.

6 They are over-influenced by the views of others.

7 They would rather talk about what they are going to do rather than do it.

8 They lack persistence and cannot work through setbacks.

9 They have a 'can't do' rather than a 'can do' attitude.

10 They work hard on what they 'can't do' rather than what they 'can do'.

11 They do not learn from their mistakes and errors.

12 They attempt to do everything themselves, refusing to ask for help.

▶

13 They reject honest and constructive criticism.

14 They lack flexibility of mind and behaviour.

15 They think in the now rather than in the future.

16 They lack social and influencing skills.

17 They cannot wait for what they want and have difficulty with delayed rewards.

18 They are pessimistic and cynical about themselves, others and their world.

19 They take advantage of others.

20 They lack integrity.

The reasons why people succeed:

1 They know what they want.

2 They are realistic in their goals.

3 They challenge themselves.

4 They live by what is possible, not by what is.

5 They have SMARTI goals.

6 They are committed.

7 They are motivated.

8 They are willing to pay the price in terms of time.

9 They will work through personal slippage and failure.

10 They reflect and learn from their errors.

11 They recognise their achievements.

12 They reward themselves for their achievements.

13 They respect their bodies regarding:

- food
- exercise

- personal hygiene
- rest.

14 They read motivational material.

15 They only compete with themselves.

16 They are inspired by others.

17 They associate with positive people.

18 They use their successes to move on.

19 They are independent of the good-will of others.

20 They are faithful in their relationships.

21 They are legitimately selfish.

PART 1

Getting started

W here to begin?

Strange but true – sometimes enthusiasm does not work in your favour. Over-enthusiasm can trap you into setting unrealistic goals for yourself. Telling yourself: 'I will be a millionaire by the age of 25' or 'CEO of a Times 100 organisation by the age of 30' is fine in fantasy but not in reality unless your surname is Gates, Buffett, Arnault or Murdoch and you have a certain family connection. So you start with mission impossible, soon discover that it's impossible and in frustration give up and become disillusioned with life.

Most of us are acorns and it takes healthy preparation before we can grow and become oaks. So in this part we spend some time orientating ourselves to what lies ahead.

Brilliant personal development is not:

- making a stack of money
- getting the corner office on the top floor in mahogany row
- being on the cover of *Time* magazine
- being chased by paparazzi.

Although some of these things might happen along the way. Brilliant personal development is a very simple concept:

Being the best you can with what you've got.

What is a reality is that you already have all the dispositional requirements to forge ahead, but it has to be step by step. Brilliant self-development is not an all or nothing activity but operating as your best self and grasping the opportunities that you create or that are given to you along your journey. OK, so Rome wasn't built in a day, but it was built and here is how you start.

'Success is not about being the best.
Success is the process of becoming your best self.'

Sally Hogshead

CHAPTER 3

Luck or effort?

W e are starting off as we mean to go on with an activity which will help you get the most out of this chapter. It's a questionnaire and I need you to be true to yourself here, despite the fact that some of the questions may tempt you to respond in a way that will make you appear to be more socially acceptable. Resist the temptation, and answer the questions as truthfully as possible, otherwise you will have what psychologists call a FIFO – fantasy in, fantasy out.

A questionnaire

For each pair of statements, tick the one that you feel/think/ believe is more you. There are no right or wrong answers and your first response is your best response.

Please answer each pair in its own right; just because you answered a particular question in a certain way should not influence your response to any other question. Please answer all the questions.

1 ☐ A Bad luck is the main reason why things go wrong.
   ☐ B Things go wrong usually because of the results of the mistakes you make.

2 ☐ A Career success is mostly the result of the effort you put in.
   ☐ B Career success is mostly being in the right place at the right time.

3 ☐ A Some things are just meant to happen in life.
   ☐ B You can make things happen in your life.

▶

4 ☐ A You get a job if you prepare well for it.
   ☐ B You get a job if the interviewer likes you.

5 ☐ A It is no use planning your life since most things are out of your control.
   ☐ B If you plan your life there is a good chance that you can achieve most of what you want.

6 ☐ A It is what you know that counts rather than who you know.
   ☐ B It is who you know that counts rather than what you know.

7 ☐ A It is possible to almost eliminate corruption with commitment and determination.
   ☐ B Corruption is endemic and cannot be eliminated even with the best intentions.

8 ☐ A Politicians get elected on the basis of their looks and their spin.
   ☐ B Politicians get elected on the basis of their policies and their reputation.

9 ☐ A It is possible to help people to like you by your actions.
   ☐ B People either like you or they don't.

10 ☐ A You cannot change your destiny.
   ☐ B Destiny is not absolute.

Scoring:

Give yourself 1 point if you scored the following:

1B, 2A, 3B, 4A, 5B, 6A, 7A, 8B, 9A, 10B

If you scored 6 and above you have a tendency to be a HLC.

If you scored 4 and below you have a tendency to be a LLC.

Let's explain this. The questions being asked in the questionnaire elicit whether or not you feel/think/believe that you are in charge of your life – high locus of control (HLC) and can do something about it – or that your life is essentially outside your control so you have a low locus of control (LLC).

This aspect was being investigated by Julian Rutter way back in 1954 who, as a typical psychologist, divided people up into two groups:

1 Those who believed that they were able to shape their lives were thought to have a high internal locus of control (HLC).

2 Those who believed that they were unable to shape their lives were thought to have a low internal locus of control (LLC).

Our locus of control helps us to decide which forces account for our failures and our successes. Being high or low on our locus of control obviously has a direct and significant effect on whether we take risks or not, how motivated we are to attempt to do things for ourselves, our expectations in life and even our self-esteem.

If you have a low locus of control then this text, and especially the activities, are going to be hard work for you because self-help is based on the principle that one can change the status quo, develop and/or grow with personal effort plus the investment of time.

Remember the mantra at the beginning of the book ...

'If it's going to be, then it's down to me.'

It's difficult to live this mantra if one believes that everything is down to luck, destiny, your genes or your family background, education, or your current social environment – all factors outside your control.

Obviously, there is such a thing as good fortune, inheriting a better gene pool, growing up in a loving and supportive family and having influential friends. But good fortune doesn't account for all of your success. It simply provides a better starting point. What you do with your serendipity of life's advantages is up to you.

'Practice does not make perfect results; it is only perfect practice that achieves perfect results.'

Anon

A challenge

Changing your behaviour is one of the most difficult tasks you can set yourself. Just think, you have been behaving this way for most of your life and now you want to be different!

We are all creatures of habit. It's a very efficient way of living. Our brain takes in new information, we practise using it and turn it into a new habit. You can see this in many areas of your everyday life.

Just think about that first driving lesson. It all seemed so complex and frightening. How would you remember all the things you needed to do at the same time? Engine on, parking brake off, clutch in, check mirrors, signal, reach the bite, drive off. And yet now you will do all of this whilst thinking about what you are having for dinner, what is happening on the news, or even what is happening on the back seat if your children are bickering. There are many other occasions in our lives when we behave and respond to situations as if we are on automatic, even on cruise control, without even realising it.

In his 1989 study, self-help guru Dr Maxwell Maltz found that to really embed new learning we have to turn it into a habit, which means practising the new behaviours for 21 consecutive days. During those days you may find this little verse helpful:

'Watch your thoughts, for they become words.
Watch your words, for they become actions.
Watch your actions, for they become habits.
Watch your habits, for they become character.
Watch your character, for it becomes your destiny.'

Ralph Waldo Emerson, essayist and leader of the
Trancendentalist movement

Suggestions for success

Here are some suggestions to help you through and assist you in developing the skills that are important to you.

Suggestion 1

Attempt only one thing at a time. Rome certainly wasn't built in a day and nor will you be able to develop yourself in lots of ways all at once.

Suggestion 2

Be continuously conscious of your behaviour and reflect on it regularly, preferably daily, paying particular attention to when you are doing well and when things are not going so well.

Suggestion 3

Go for easy wins first. If you try something hard first and fail then you are likely to give up with the rest of your agenda. Be gentle with yourself and get some easy runs on the board. This will give you the confidence necessary to keep you motivated. Once you have the confidence then change tack and apply 'Grandma's law' (see Chapter 1).

Suggestion 4

Set yourself reasonable and sensible targets. Occasionally we allow our enthusiasm to outrun us: make 20 new network friends this month; date five people in a month; volunteer to make two presentations at the board meeting this month; get to my ideal body weight within a month. Unrealistic targets bring realistic failures. In reality, your zeal has zapped you.

 'You don't need to see the whole staircase but just take the first step.'

Martin Luther King, civil rights leader

Suggestion 5

Allow for and anticipate some slippage, especially when you are under pressure or in new situations. We revert to what we instinctively know because that is when we are most comfortable. Many Britons have died in car accidents in France because intuitively, in a sudden, dangerous situation, the driver has automatically responded by driving on the left-hand side of the road. Thankfully your slippage won't be as dramatic, but do expect some occasional slippage back into your old ways. Treat your slippage as a learning opportunity. Don't beat yourself up; it's only a temporary setback.

'They who struggle and yet fail today, can live to fight another day.'

Erasmus, 1542

Babies, when learning to walk, in an attempt to get somewhere quickly will often deliberately revert to crawling because it's easier, faster, more effective and they know they can do it. However, babies never, never give up in their attempts to walk.

When you realise your lapse in motivation, commitment and behaviour then consider it as a 'rest day' and get back on track tomorrow. Jugglers, especially when they are learning or developing a new trick, have a great saying: 'If you ain't dropping you ain't juggling.' Slippage goes with the territory of self-development so, 'If you ain't slipping you ain't developing'!

Trite but right: even two steps forward and one step back still makes one ahead of where you were.

 **tip**

Take slippage as a sign of progress and let it motivate you to get back on track.

Suggestion 6

Be satisfied with small wins. Massive changes in a person's behaviour can be achieved, but they are usually associated with actual or anticipated trauma. Sometimes a major change can occur after a significant emotional event, but then again it requires an external agency. Be satisfied with small wins because most of us are not lucky enough to win the lottery.

Suggestion 7

Reward yourself when you achieve a specific target. Alright, I know that humans are far superior to laboratory rats, pigeons and monkeys but reward for achievement definitely works for them and it will definitely work for you. Rewards work best when they are specific to you. If you like wine then a six pack of beers is not going to cut it.

Rewards should be graded as well, for example (providing they work for you) ice-cream for a small success, a bottle of wine to enjoy with your partner for the next, then a meal out, then a weekend break and for the big one a two-week cruise or some time on the Orient Express. As you enjoy your reward at the beginning, middle and end tell yourself, 'I am doing this because I have just achieved … and I deserve it.'

Suggestion 8

Work with a friend who wants to achieve the same things as you; essentially we are pack animals, enjoying the company of people like ourselves. It is true, as four young men sung half a century ago, that: 'You get by with a little help from your friends.'[1]

---

1 'With a Little Help from My Friends' is a song written by John Lennon and Paul McCartney, released on the Beatles' album *Sgt. Pepper's Lonely Hearts Club Band* in 1967.

Suggestion 9

Keep a written list of all your successes, then from time to time, especially when things get difficult, read through what you have achieved, reflect on your successes, rejoice and feel proud. Achievements are energising, particularly in those inevitable 'down' moments. Achievements are yours: you achieved them and no one can take them away from you.

 **activity**

List all the things that you can do now which you could not do three years ago. You will be amazed at how your talents and abilities have grown. If you have difficulty doing this you were very wise to buy this text!

Suggestion 10

Well not quite a suggestion but a possible challenge. As you change you will find that others will be surprised at the 'new you'. Some will prefer the 'old' you and social pressure, even from close friends, may be brought to bear to keep you the way you were.

When we were teenagers we all went through that cloning stage of strident individuality paradoxically resulting in us all looking, dressing and speaking alike. We adjust when we discover the real face of maturity behind all the teenage acne. Good friends will support you as you grow and develop. However, it's a very common phenomenon that most people you know will wish for you to be successful *but* not more successful than they are!

brilliant recap

● Attempt only one thing at a time.

● Review your behaviour regularly.

● Do the easy things first.

● Keep your goals reasonable.

● Anticipate occasional slippage.

● Be satisfied with small changes.

● Reward yourself.

● Work with a friend.

● List and review your achievements.

● Realise that friends might not always support you.

CHAPTER 4

Discovering you

A s with every journey or project, the best place to start is finding out where we are now. Which in this case means gaining a thorough understanding of who *you* are.

Most of us think of ourselves through the labels that have been donated to us by others. Some may be true; most should be tested because they tend to be based on the roles that we play each day: wife, son, mother, brother, friend, employee, manager, etc. These are easy tags to give people, but you have to look behind the descriptor and see the person who is deciding how that role should be played.

It is only by knowing who we are that we can know what we want to become. With this deeper understanding of ourselves comes the ability to see clearly the opportunities available to us.

Self-knowledge means being honest with ourselves and recognising both our strengths and our blind spots (French for weaknesses!). Remember that in a way success in life is the reverse of in school where we had to work very hard on those things that did not come naturally such as maths or spelling. In life a better strategy is to be continually playing to your strengths, whilst doing all that you can to ensure that your weaknesses do not act as a roadblock along the route to success.

'I do not believe that you should devote overly much effort to correcting your weaknesses. Rather I believe that the highest success in living and the deepest emotional satisfaction comes from building and using your signature strengths.'

Martin Seligman, psychologist

Your resources

Let's start with 'Who am I?' and 'What inner resources do I have?' From this base camp we can climb to achieve our personal heights, moving upward on our journey of discovery, making choices, developing ourselves and enjoying a sense of satisfaction when we make the summit.

Usually, because we are too busy with the 'doing' part of our lives, we do not take time out to think about who we are and what we have. Most people if you asked them, 'Who are you?' would usually put external labels on themselves rather than describing who they really are. For instance you might say of yourself:

'I am single, I live in Woodside, I work as a programmer for an engineering firm, I have a dog and I am interested in astronomy, I am slightly overweight but I am working on it, I have a daughter. Let me tell you about my daughter ...'

All of this, of course, is absolutely true but it describes the person in terms of marital status, geography, employment, pets, interests and body image, and suggests someone who is not comfortable talking about themselves.

This is like restricting our view to the state of the car body not the engine, the farm and not the farmer, the photograph not the person. Of course you can make inferences – a low, wide and two-seater car probably has a racing engine, a beautifully kept farm indicates a well-organised farmer, from a photograph one can infer body shape, age and perhaps even social status – but they would all be inferences and assumptions. We know from experience how unreliable assumptions are and how wide of the mark are the impressions formed from the dog breeder's glossy brochure.

In working on and understanding ourselves we must mine below the surface level at which we are comfortable. Then comes the confidence to show to the world who we really are and those things of which we are really capable.

There are large filing cabinets of psychology papers gathering dust, which all come to roughly the same conclusion: 'The best indicator of future performance is past performance.' So most of our navel-gazing will be looking back at our lives.

Much of the way we are today reflects the way in which we developed during childhood. It was Ignatius who said: 'Give me a child until he is seven, and I will give you the man.' This is true: the buds we have in childhood usually blossom in adulthood.

Some activities

Now, as you were warned (promised?) earlier on, we come to some activities for you to complete and brood on. Take your time over these activities otherwise you will wear yourself out. After each activity do spend some time reflecting on them. You might like to make notes on any insights that you have gained in your log book. You may find some activities will be more challenging or interesting than others but to get the best results please do all of them.

brilliant activity

Serendipity or 'What did I receive without much work?'

1 Given my family background what advantages did I gain?

(a)

(b)

(c)

(d)

(e)

2 What advantages are there in being male/female?

(a)

(b)

(c)

(d)

(e)

3 What are the advantages that my personality provides for me?

(a)

(b)

(c)

(d)

(e)

4 Given my IQ and my EQ what advantages do I have?

    (a)

    (b)

    (c)

    (d)

    (e)

5 What can I do with minimum effort that others seem to find difficult?

    (a)

    (b)

    (c)

    (d)

    (e)

6 How have I been helped by family and friends?

    (a)

    (b)

    (c)

    (d)

    (e)

7 What were my early hopes that have helped my life to date?

(a)

(b)

(c)

(d)

(e)

8 In my leisure and in my career what do I really enjoy doing?

(a)

(b)

(c)

d)

(e)

9 What has my health enabled me to do?

(a)

(b)

(c)

(d)

(e)

10 What advantages did school and/or college give me?

(a)

(b)

(c)

(d)

(e)

12 Besides my own efforts, to what would I attribute my early successes?

(a)

(b)

(c)

(d)

(e)

Reflection points

All these aspects about yourself came mostly for free. You can call it fate, karma or serendipity but they all came with very little effort on your part.

What is helpful here is that knowing the 'gifts' that you have been given keeps you from thinking that you are better than you are, it keeps you grounded in reality and enables you to better appreciate the achievements you've had to work at.

Reflection 1

Some of the questions will reveal more about yourself than

others. Review all your answers to the above questions and then complete the following statement:

In my early life I was fortunate in that _____

_____

Reflection 2
What advantages here should you leverage to your gain? What are the springboards of your life up until now?

 'By three methods we may learn wisdom: first, by reflection, which is noblest; second, by imitation, which is easiest; and third by experience, which is the bitterest.'

Confucius

Activity: when I was young

As we have noted, the best indicator of future performance is past performance. For the majority of us, our main interests and predilections mature rather than change as we grow older. Even if life forces us to travel in a different direction we ease back to our true selves as soon as we possibly can. Think of these preferences as your life anchors: tides and storms of your experience attempt to batter you but your anchor keeps you in place ready to sail with your preferences when the tide is right.

This activity is designed to discover if, when we were young, there were early signs of what direction in life we might follow. A friend of mine who is a priest remembers 'baptising' his sister's doll at a very early age. Susan Hill, the bestselling author and my contemporary at university, was writing stories at a very early age, so it was not surprising that she wrote and had published her first novel *The Enclosure* when she was just 15 years old.

So here are some orientation questions that might prompt the discovery or recognition of some reoccurring themes in your life.

brilliant activity

When I was small, people used to say that I was very good at

_____

The very first compliment that I can remember was about my ability to

_____

Other compliments I received during my childhood have been for

_____

When I was a child, I could spend hours doing

_____

My interests and hobbies when I was small were

_____

When I was a child, I daydreamed about being

_____

When I was a child, the thing I was most proud of was

_____

My childhood heroes were (give brief reasons why)

_____

The subjects at school that I found easy were

_____

My school reports usually said that I was

_____

My role in the family was

_____

My siblings would ask me to help them with/when

_____

My parents always thought I would

_____

In reviewing your answers are there any recurrent themes? What has persisted from your childhood into your current life? What do you like to do during your leisure and in your career to date that originated in your past? How has your childhood affected or influenced the person you are today, the relationships you enjoy and the career that you have chosen?

 'The child is the father of the man.'

Sigmund Freud, Austrian neurologist and psychoanalyst

Activity: your history

Yes, of course we are a product of our genes and our genetic history, but here we must do some serious work on our own history as our environment also has an effect on who we are. So we begin with an activity called life line:

The horizontal axis of this graph represents your life from when you were born on the left to where you are now on the right. The vertical axis shows your emotional line, which shows how you have felt at different points in your life; above the line are the good times and below the line are the hard times. The higher above the line the better it was for you and the lower below the line the worse it was for you

Nobody's life is a straight line of meritocracy: we all have ups and downs, successes and failures, highs and lows. Here is an example of an early part of life:

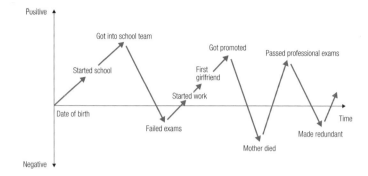

Life line: stage 1

As you can see you are going to need a very large sheet of paper so I suggest you join lots of A4 sheets together rather like a scroll than a book with sequential pages.

Now develop your life line graph. The more you put into it the more useful it will be. Put in as much detail as possible of your life's journey to date until today.

In another colour, using the same graph, superimpose your 'health line' above and below the line reflecting your state of health at the time.

Finally, in yet another colour superimpose your 'relationship(s) line' again above and below the line to reflect how happy you were (or were not) with relationships with the significant others in your life.

Most of us live in one-year windows: we remember the past six months and plan ahead for the next six. This activity enables you to see the whole of your life spread out before you and get some perspective on what is happening.

Life line: stage 2

The first thing we need to do is interrogate your life line to see what it can teach us. So ask yourself the following questions of the overall graph:

Are any patterns emerging?

- Is there a span of time when something happens to take you off on a new tangent/direction or adventure?

- If there are patterns, what could this tell you about your life and/or yourself?

- If there are patterns then for most people life comes in waves of five to seven years. If this is you then where are you in your current 'wave' and what do you want to achieve in your next 'wave'?

- Are there periods of success followed by downtimes or is it mixed?

- Did you anticipate the major changes or did they take you by surprise?

- Were you proactive or reactive?

- Did you ever have a plan for yourself?

- Did it go to plan or were there some surprises?

- Is there any relationship between your life line, health line and relationship line?

- Does one line 'push' the other or does it 'follow' certain events?

Now we will look at the implications your life line has on your future.

 **activity**

Above the line

Look at all the items and events above the line and ask yourself the following questions. Be as specific as you can (this is a good activity to record in your log book):

- What motivated you to initiate this event?

- Did you plan it or did it just happen?

- What, if anything, did you do to achieve this event in your life?
- What, if any, risks did you take to achieve this event?
- Why was the event enjoyable?
- What made it enjoyable?
- Who did you tell about it and why them?
- What were the feelings/emotions you enjoyed?
- Who were you with during the event?
- What part, if any, did they play to make the event enjoyable?
- Did this event change you in any way?

Now write in your development log book the answer/reflection to the question:

I have been most happy in my life when I _____
because _____

Now list what you have achieved so far; list as many things as you can think of that you have achieved, or you are proud of, with regard to:

- your family, friends and other personal relationships
- your career
- your material wealth and possessions
- your spiritual development.

If you wish you can also review:

- your health, personal development and learning
- your 'inner' or psychological development.

Below the line
Now look where your line has fallen below the average line. In as much detail as possible – unless it is too hurtful to go there – ask yourself these questions. Again it's useful to use as much detail as possible: it will maximise learning and possibly help you to avoid the same mistakes again.

- Why was it painful?
- Did it just happen or did you contribute in some way to the event?   ▷

- What were the emotions that you felt?
- Who did you discuss the event with and why them?
- Who helped you recover or gave you advice to help you move on?
- What did you learn from the experience?
- How, if at all, did your behaviour change?

Having done this, complete the statement:
In the future I must be aware of _____

_____

Now, having reviewed the 'ups' and 'downs' in your life in considerable detail, we can move on to the next stage.

 'When we begin to take our futures less seriously, it means we are ceasing to be afraid of them.'

Katherine Mansfield, author

Life line: stage 3

You now have a list of achievements. But what might you want for the future? In your log book complete the following phrase:

> Given the totality of my experience in life to date, in the future it would be sensible for me to _____
>
> _____

If you wish you can ask the same question of:

- your health and relationships
- your personal development
- your career development
- your material aspirations.

Again record your decisions in your log book.

 'The best moments of your life are when you are being your authentic self.

Then you are in your creation and doing what you love to do.'

Don Miguel Ruiz, Mexican author

Activity: life influences

Let's now turn to the 'influences' on your life. Consider the events/people that have influenced and/or helped or had a significant effect on your life up until now (e.g. parents, siblings, family members, significant others, managers, teachers, coaches, friends, etc.). Complete the following table:

	Names/events	How were you influenced?
1.1		
1.2		
1.3		
1.4		
1.5		

Then consider your major achievements/golden moments in your life to date:

	Name/events
2.1	
2.2	
2.3	
2.4	
2.5	

Now consider the times that you have been most successful/happy in your life:

	Names/events	Reason/because
3.1		
3.2		
3.3		
3.4		
3.5		

Remember the risks you have taken in your life:

	Risk	The reward for me was?
4.1		
4.2		
4.3		
4.4		
4.5		

Consider when and how you have helped others:

	Individual	Helped in what way?
5.1		
5.2		
5.3		
5.4		
5.5		

 activity

Updating your log book

Write in your log book, or list them here, at least three or four things from the above activity which may have a bearing on your future

1 _____

2 _____

3 _____

4 _____

Activity: develop a personal mind map

It is not easy to say who we are in a succinct way so in this activity there is a structure to assist you to explore who you are, developed by Tony Buzan. He calls it 'mind mapping'.

You could think of yourself in four main categories, namely your:

● skills

● traits or personality

● values

● reputation.

Draw them as balloons and then you may want to draw smaller balloons showing a sub-section or an outcome of that particular balloon (category).

So, for example, if you have skills in the first balloon it would look like this:

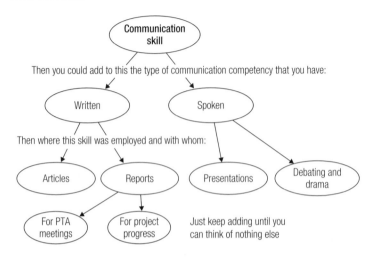

When you do this for yourself, the larger the sheet the more balloons you can add so that you have as much information about yourself as possible. See if you can obtain some A1 paper or flip chart paper and attach it to a suitable wall. You will be surprised at how much you can expand your mind map.

This will be a challenging but interesting activity. It will cause you to think really deeply about yourself. Because it is difficult, since you don't often reflect on who you are, you might find enlisting some friends to help is useful (perhaps even have fun doing each person's balloon 'map' in turn). If you do this you must tell them to be very honest with you – and that you will still be friends after the activity!

Activity: your 'I am' statement

Now, using all the information that you have gathered about yourself from your mind map, construct a 30–50 word statement about yourself, including as much as you can in each category.

 **example**

For example, using the mind map opposite, this person might describe themselves in the following way:

Skills

I am a very creative person, mainly in the arts – particularly in music and poetry – who is blessed with good teaching skills, reflecting my ability to give excellent presentations based upon my research and my love of being practical.

Traits

I am an extrovert by nature, which means I am friendly and outward going. Being empathetic, but in a down-to-earth and practical way, friends trust me and say that I give good advice.

Values

I consider myself to be an honest and fair person who values their independence and who is also committed, especially to my family and friends. I like to work hard which sometimes means I can be competitive – I always strive to be the best I can.

Reputation

I have a reputation for being professional in my dealings with other people. Some would say that I am highly competitive and quick to see opportunities for myself and others; friends say I am kind and always the eternal optimist.

Being able to understand and describe yourself in this way will be a tremendous help when you come to developing confidence in yourself to develop and grow. I hope you can see how this process reflects a much better understanding of yourself than saying 'single, living in Woodside, etc.'

Activity: select and use your 'I am'

Develop a series of 'I am' statements around that which you wish to become. Below are some examples of positive statements:

- I am good person.
- I have integrity.
- I do what is ethically right and good.
- Whatever life puts before me it will be a useful experience that will make me stronger, wiser and more tolerant.
- I am strong enough to understand and make allowances for other people's weaknesses, and their behaviour towards me.
- Other people's behaviour is about them, not me.
- I focus on the joy of living my life and helping others where and when I can.
- I am what I eat and drink, so I eat and drink good things.
- I am what I watch and play and listen, so I watch and play and listen to good, positive things.
- I take exercise which I enjoy. I walk when I don't need to drive or take the bus or train.
- I smile and laugh whenever I can – life is good. Getting caught in the rain reminds me that it is good to be alive to feel it.
- I forgive other people. Deep down everyone is a good person, just like me.
- I am a compassionate, loving and caring person.

Say your 'I am' statements out loud and with conviction. If possible, find somewhere where you can shout them as loud as you can. It's an invigorating experience and helps to embed the statements into the subconscious, where they will take root and grow in strength. As this happens, you will see how your behaviour will change to reflect them.

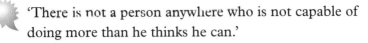

'There is not a person anywhere who is not capable of doing more than he thinks he can.'

Henry Ford

'He who gains a victory over other men is strong; but he who gains a victory over himself is all-powerful.'

Lao-Tzu, founder of Taoism

'No man is free who is not master of himself ... Is freedom anything else than the power of living as we choose?'

Epictetus, Phrygian philosopher

'You are already complete. You just don't know it.'

Zen saying

'Ignorance is not bliss. Ignorance is ignorance.'

John Laws, Australian radio presenter

CHAPTER 5

Discovering your core beliefs

Our core beliefs are at the root of everything we do. They influence how we think about and behave towards ourselves, others and the world around us.

The brain develops these beliefs to help and protect us. Formed through our life experiences, especially from childhood and adolescence, they are like an operating manual. They are often extremely rigid and resistant to change. Sometimes they are quite simply inappropriate and the resulting behaviour works against us.

We tend to operate and make our important life decisions under the influence of our core beliefs. Many of our values – which we will be considering in the next section – are usually driven by our core beliefs. In all likelihood you may have no idea what those beliefs are because they will be safely buried in your subconscious. So before we can understand what is driving us it's vital to discover what our beliefs are and whether any of them are out of date or misinformed.

To do this we will use a technique called 'laddering'. Laddering is used a great deal in psychotherapy because there is no contamination from the psychologist. Laddering is also employed in market research because it is to manufacturers' and retailers' advantage to know why we make certain buying decisions.[1]

---

1 As a result of laddering techniques used in market research, cigarette packets became white; Shell changed its logo to green; and even chickens were allowed out for an hour a day to be 'free range'. Fast-food outlets are still doing their best to appear organic and healthy.

In laddering you just keep probing, asking yourself 'Why?' or 'What does that do for me?' until you can go no further. It is rather like the way two year olds interrogate us with their ubiquitous and repetitive 'Why?' They ladder up on each answer you give until, with exasperation, you cannot go any further and blurt out something like 'Because that is just the way that it is!'

▶ brilliant example

Here is an example of 'laddering' working on a statement (S) and Q&A (Q) technique:

(S) I like low-fat milk.

(Q) Why?

(A) Well I prefer that taste.

(Q) Why is that important to you?

(A) It's not so creamy.

(Q) Why is that important to you?

(A) Because it has no fat in it.

(Q) Why is that important to you?

(A) Because fat is bad for you.

(Q) Why is that important to you?

(A) Because I want to be healthy.

(Q) Why is that important to you?

(A) It just is.

Here you can see the 'laddering up' until the steps just run out and there is nowhere else to go. It's here that the core belief is revealed: **it is important to be healthy**.

So low-fat milk is promoted not because of taste, or cost or because it will make a better cup of tea, but because it is healthy.

 **example**

Here's another example:

(Q) What do you do?

(A) I am a nurse.

(Q) Why did you choose that profession?

(A) I like people.

(Q) What does that do for you?

(A) I get a buzz out of helping people.

(Q) Why is that important to you?

(A) Because it is the right thing to do.

(Q) Why is it right?

(A) It just is.

Core belief: **it is important to help others**.

So employment advertising for nurse applicants places an emphasis on how caring for others enables personal satisfaction.

What are your core beliefs?

Here are some questions you could ask yourself to discover your core beliefs:

- What do you enjoy doing in your leisure time?
- What do you like about your partner?
- Why do you vote the way you do?
- What was the biggest risk that you have ever taken?

- What are you most proud of in your life and work?
- What is you favourite film/book?
- Tell me about an important argument in the past that you just had to have.
- What has been your most significant emotional experience?
- What sort of presents would you prefer to buy for people?
- What has been the hardest decision that you ever had to make?
- Should you die tomorrow what three things would you like to be remembered for?

Laddering is an important way of understanding yourself and others because it gives you deep insight into your core values and what makes you (and those around you) 'tick'.

 **brilliant** example

Core beliefs

Here are a few example core beliefs – you will discover more as you embark on the activity. Mostly they can be prefaced with 'always':

- be responsible
- be industrious
- be right
- be careful
- be respectful (of my elders)
- be modest
- be honest
- be healthy
- be spiritual
- be logical
- be in control
- be principled
- be humble
- be the best (or do my best) at all times
- be just
- be tough
- be independent
- be thrifty
- be helpful
- be faithful and loyal
- be cautious
- be generous
- be modest
- be creative.

Core beliefs usually come prefaced by 'I must/ought/should' and have a suffix along the lines of 'because it is right/ it helps me/ my parents taught me/ it makes sense/ that is what I believe/ it is in the Holy Book of my faith'.

Core beliefs can also be negative and damaging. These are again prefaced by 'I am' and sometimes can have the suffix 'because'.

brilliant example

Here are some of the negative 'I am' beliefs:

- not good enough (incompetent)
- not good enough (unlovable)
- unwanted
- stupid
- untidy
- hopeless
- selfish
- imperfect

- silly
- lazy
- different
- defective
- imperfect
- bad
- powerless
- not safe.

As small children, if we suffer inadequate parenting, abuse or shame and we attempt to make sense of what is happening to us using 'because' – 'I am not like others', 'life is hard', 'I cannot please my parents' – then we, unfortunately, later use such statements to help us make sense of the world around us.

Facing the same environment each and every day, these beliefs become embedded deep in our psyche and can later have a detrimental effect on our self-esteem and our subsequent behaviour. Because at a deep level a person thinks – knows – that they are powerless, they don't even try to stand up for their rights. These core beliefs are the subconscious dams that hold us back on fulfilling our potential. Such statements rattle round in our heads whenever we are motivated to develop ourselves.

Such beliefs are independent of your analytical mind, so it is difficult to resolve them with reason alone or employ your analytical skills. We will examine how to deal with these inappropriate beliefs later, but the good news is that once you recognise that you have been the victim of such negative beliefs, and you recognise that they are part of your early life, you can choose whether or not to keep, dispose of or respond to them, and act accordingly

Usually we have about six or seven core beliefs. Sometimes they conflict with each other, so for example, while we might agree that it is important to be thrifty, healthy and independent, we also go on shopping sprees, indulge in fast food and usually agree with what our peer group values.

 'To know and not to do is not to know.'

Zen saying

 activity

Make a list of all the things you have done in the past six months that support your core belief. If this is difficult then think of 10 actions you have undertaken when you were challenged or had to make an ethical or difficult decision.

Having done this it is then back to the drawing board to reflect on what this might tell you about your important beliefs. It is easy to fool yourself and think you are better than you actually are.

Share your core beliefs with a friend who will be honest and give you reliable feedback. (It could be very helpful for you to tell the friend that you will still value their friendship after you have had the discussion!)

'Never let your sense of morals keep you from doing what is right.'

Isaac Asimov, author

'It is not a value at all which has not some influence upon the actions of him who holds it.'

William Kingdom Clifford, English mathematician

brilliant recap

- To really understand ourselves we need to discover our core beliefs.

- Core beliefs are very important because they determine our important decisions right down to the trivia of what we buy at the supermarket.

- 'Laddering' is an easy way of discovering our core beliefs.

- Some core beliefs can be damaging and it's important to recognise them so that we can discard them if they are unhealthy.

CHAPTER 6

Discovering your values

alues secretly pervade and underpin the whole of our life. Everyone has values that dominate their behaviour and, interestingly, we are hardly conscious of them as our values are the ghosts behind most of our decisions. But it is rare for us, when thinking about options and decisions, to identify them by going through the following process:

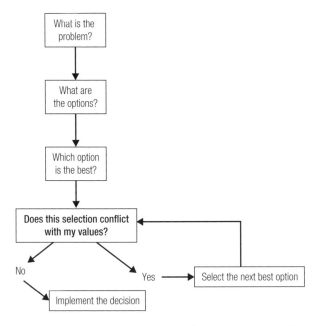

Our values guide us to act in a certain way; they are the quiet voice of our conscience.

Until we are aware of our values, we are quite often oblivious as to how deeply they affect our behaviour throughout our lives both at work and at play. One example would be how we respond to the rules which form part of our lives: the laws society expects us to obey, the behaviour expected of us by our family, friends or colleagues.

Rules tell us what to do and direct us in certain behaviours. However, if they are not aligned with our values they become obligations and are liable to be broken, whether from a sense of rebelliousness or simply knowing that you disagree with them. And when rules are broken they are usually enforced by some form of punishment.

As the underlying driver of our behaviour, values have an enormous influence on us in numerous ways, affecting:

- the image of ourselves that we wish to project to the world
- how we make a decision about what is right and what is wrong
- whether or not we feel guilty
- whether or not we will be charitable
- whether or not we like someone
- our choice of partner
- how we rear our children
- our loyalty to individuals and organisations
- where and the way we live
- how we spend our disposable income
- the career we choose
- the sort of organisation we like to work for
- our political allegiance
- what we do with our leisure time
- the things we purchase

- the way we dress
- the TV programmes and films we watch
- the music we listen to
- the material we read.

It may sound contradictory, but we can also have negative values. These are values which encourage us to break the golden rule of treating others as we would wish to be treated ourselves. In this section we will concentrate on the original meaning of 'value', with a value being something of worth and accepted by society.

'I have never been able to separate my personal values from business values. I am mystified by the fact that the business world is apparently proud to be seen as hard and uncaring and detached from human values.'

Anita Roddick, founder of the Body Shop

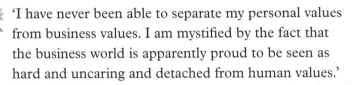

brilliant tip

A good starting point to become clear about what your values are is to look at how you spend your disposable time and income and ask yourself: 'Why do I do this? At a deep level, what do I gain from this?' Obviously when the restraints of life's handcuffs are off – work, family duties, social requirements, sleep, etc. – then doing what we like in our 'own' time must reflect what we enjoy doing, which is driven by our values. So a quick review of your diary and personal expenditure should prove to be a revealing insight into your values.

Remember that each activity could be fulfilling a number of values. Take, for example, making wooden bowls on a lathe, which could satisfy any of the following values:

- It is important to be creative.
- I feel good when I reach a level of adeptness in an art.

- It is important for me to be perfect and making a perfect bowl is a good challenge.

- It is important for me to be generous so I give my bowls away.

- It is important for me to fill my time doing something useful.

- It is important for me to be challenged so I work with different and difficult wood.

- It is important for me to be close to my son and this is something which we can do together.

- It is important for me to win so every year I enter my best bowl in the county show.

- It is important for me to enjoy good health and this provides relief from my stressful job.

- It is important for me to do something which maximises my income from my free time.

Where do values come from?

Not many values are hard-wired, rather they are inculcated by our family, especially our parents, those who are emotionally significant for us at a young age and our social conditioning. Interestingly, our values are formed very early so few of us by the time we are able to drive do not have the value 'I must not speed' when driving, for example.

Right or wrong

In an intellectual sense values are neither right nor wrong – they just are. They reflect the sum of the individual's reflection on their experience as they develop their understanding of life and their world. It is worth noting that it is estimated that in the Western world those under 25 have most of their values shaped by the media, particularly through television. Social networking sites also have a large part to play.

An individual's values stay with them for life unless they suffer some unfortunate traumatic event. What do you think might have happened to the person who says 'I trust everyone but I always lock my car'?

Logic and values

What is interesting about our values is that they are not dependent upon logic. Logic helps in giving direction, and in the way we make decisions. Nevertheless, in the end, it is our value system that is our 'choice compass' that prompts and guides our decisions. After we make that decision our logic kicks in to justify the choice.

 **example**

The situation:

Two people, Mr A and Mr B, both want to purchase a car.

The purchasers:

Are the same age, same gender, same background, same education, both married, both in the same job in very similar organisations, and both with the same amount of cash to buy a car, etc. - i.e. identical people in all environmental respects.

Value differences:

Mr A values individualism, independence, competitiveness, excitement and recognition.

Mr B values traditionalism, security, physical comfort, stability and functionality.

Question:

Who would buy the black estate and who would buy the red sports car?

Logic says 'I need a car for transport' but individual values will determine the vehicle. However, what is very interesting is the 'why' of the purchase. When we are challenged for an explanation of our choice we are all absolute masters at providing irrefutable logical reasoning to justify ourselves. But even so it would be unusual to do this on the basis of our values. Can you imagine hearing someone tell you:

● 'I bought my sports car because I am an individualist
   and very competitive, always seeking the excitement
   that independence brings; besides I like to be noticed.'
   or

● 'I bought my estate because a larger car is safer and has
   a lower insurance rating. It was a good deal and it should
   hold its value, besides I feel it reflects a certain gravitas and
   stability.'

But once you understand how your values are driving your behaviour you have access to a new level of control and a powerful way of making choices about what you are doing and how you are doing it.

Values at work

Organisations also have values and, for your sense of job satisfaction, it is absolutely vital that your values are aligned with your company.

You can easily spot if this isn't the case. If you are in a position where you have the right skill set and are well remunerated but also suffer from a high level of stress and stress-related illnesses such as back pain, stomach upset, fatigue, skin problems and high blood pressure then you are probably working for a company that does not share your values.

On the other hand, if your values are in sync you will find your levels of job satisfaction and performance soar and you will be in a great position for the opportunities available to you within that company.

In the same way that you can uncover your personal values through looking at how you use your income and time, a company's values can be uncovered by looking at its website. This is an important exercise to complete when you are thinking about your next job. If you don't, you may find yourself out of the frying pan and into the fire. Most companies publish their values on their websites and/or in their annual reports. With a little digging you could find the information you need.

brilliant example

Here are some examples of company values:

- integrity
- innovation
- fun
- leadership
- team orientation
- customer satisfaction
- profit
- treat others with fairness, respect, dignity

- high ethical standards
- respect and compliance with the law
- environmental respect
- safe working practice
- local community focused
- exceeds customer needs

Sometimes you get a clever acronym. My local hospital has STRIVE which stands for:

Service, **T**eamwork, **R**espect, **I**ntegrity, **V**alidity, **E**xcellence.

You might think that these are all 'fat' words and far too general, but they give you an idea of what company values, broadly speaking, may be. Of course what organisations say and what they do (remember Enron in the US and Barclays in the UK) can be very different. Now to some activity work to discover what our values may be.

 activity

Discovering your values

Look at the list below and consider which values are important to you:

Advancement	Fun	Reflection
Aesthetics	Functionality	Reputation
Achievement	Generosity	Rewards
Appreciation	Glamour	Riches
Beauty	High earnings	Rigour
Challenges	Independence	Risk
Change	Individual reward	Routines
Choice	Innovation	Security
Community	Justice	Serenity
Competition	Knowledge	Service
Culture	Kudos	Simplicity
Decision sharing	Leadership	Sincerity
Determination	Learning	Sophistication
Direction	Opportunity	Spirituality
Education	Options	Stability
Effort	Permanence	Status
Enjoyment	Personal growth	Structure
Enthusiasm	Physical comfort	Thinking
Excitement	Planning	Tradition
Fame	Pleasure	Trust
Fairness	Power	Understanding
Fashion	Pragmatism	Variety
Fixed rules	Precision	Vision
Flexibility	Professionalism	Work
Freedom	Quality	
Friendship	Recognition	

From this list choose your five most important values and rank them in order:

1st _____

2nd _____

3rd _____

4th _____

5th _____

If you have a value which is not on the list above and is in your top five then please add it to your rankings.

 **activity**

The either or activity

You might think this activity is a bit frivolous but it's a great way to release your subconscious mind so that, as you work through it, your values will begin to surface. You can do this by yourself, but it's much more fun to turn it into a 'game' with two or three friends.

Instructions

Circle a word from each word pair below that you feel or think is more like you most of the time. There are no right or wrong answers. Complete the list of 20 as quickly as possible. Once you have finished, if you are doing this with someone else, wait for the other person to finish their list.

The list

Preface the following word pairs with 'Are you ...':

A summer or a winter person   A savoury or a sweet person

Analogue or digital   A lake or a river

A cat or a dog person   A bee or a butterfly

▶

A train or a bus	Twitter or Facebook
Fact or fiction	Dolphin or eagle
Sun or moon	Paper or wood
Apple or tomato	Pen or pencil
Emerald or pearl	Gas or electric
Ballet or opera	Knife or fork
Dictionary or thesaurus	Director or producer

And now ...

The purpose of this activity is to dig down into the deep values that are motivating your life: your core values. To do this we are going to use the laddering technique (see Chapter 5). For each word you have identified ask 'Why is this important?' and for every answer keep asking 'Why?' until you reach the point of saying 'Because it is'. Then you'll have found a core value. For example:

Q Dictionary or thesaurus?

A Thesaurus.

Q Why is that important?

A Because I like to extend my vocabulary by seeing which other words mean the same thing.

Q Why is that important?

A Because it's fun to play around with words and see how different synonyms affect a sentence.

Q Why is that important?

A Because I enjoy using words and increasing my knowledge of them.

Q Why is that important?

A Because it can change the way you look at things.

Q Why is that important?

A Because things can become more interesting if you at look them from different angles.

Q Why is that important?

A Because it keeps life fresh and exciting and open to new possibilities.

Q Why is that important?

A Because otherwise we stagnate.

Q Why is that important?

A Because life is too precious to stagnate.

Q Why is that important?

A Because it just is.

So here the over-arching value is: **life should be a journey of continuous learning and personal development.**

Notice the 'should' in the concluding statement: most values are expressed in modal verbs of obligation such as 'should', 'must' and 'ought'. When you catch yourself saying, 'I should/must/ought' then beneath that statement lies a value.

If you worked on the above activity in pairs you will find dramatic differences in the core values underpinning your choices, even if you chose the same word pairs initially.

 activity

Proverb confusion

In the following pairs of proverbs, in most cases one counteracts the other. Select which of each pair resonates more for you. As with the activity before, it is best to do this quickly.

1	Attack is the best form of defence	v	Everything comes to he who waits
2	We are all equal	v	It takes all sorts to make a world

3	The devil is in the detail	v	Ignorance is bliss
4	Look before you leap	v	Throw caution to the wind
5	Many hands make light work	v	Too many cooks spoil the broth
6	Haste makes waste	v	He who hesitates is lost
7	Give credit where credit is due	v	Flattery will get you nowhere
8	Waste not, want not	v	Eat drink and be merry, for tomorrow we die
9	Easy come, easy go	v	Early to bed and early to rise, makes a man healthy, wealthy and wise
10	It's never too late	v	It's no use locking the stable door after the horse has bolted

Having selected 10 proverbs, what might this suggest about your values? For example: 'Haste makes waste' could have several meanings such as 'I must be cautious and not take risks' or 'I must be determined and persistent.' Use laddering to reveal the value in more specific terms.

When you have completed these activities, reflect on your thoughts and then rank order your seven most important values.

1 _____

2 _____

3 _____

4 _____

5 _____

6 _____

7 _____

Questions of discovery

Now you are in a position to ask yourself the following questions:

- If these are my values how have they influenced the decisions I have made in my life so far and what are the possible implications for the future?

- How can I use the knowledge of my values in future, especially when making major life decisions?

- Have I been conscious of these values in the way they may have shaped my life?

- Have those decisions been satisfactory?

- What are my learning points here?

- Should I rethink my values, re-rank them or change them for the future regarding what I want to achieve?

'I think somehow we learn who we really are and then live with that decision.'

Eleanor Roosevelt, civil rights advocate

'Try not to become a man of success but rather to become a man of value.'

Albert Einstein, physicist

 **brilliant** recap

- We will always have values so it's important to recognise them as the foundation supporting most of our decisions.

- We become stronger and more integrated when we are aware of our values, helping us to avoid knee-jerk decision making.

- Recognising that values can be different to our own enables us to understand people better, improve our emotional intelligence and anticipate the decisions they might make.

- Most great figures (past or present) have stuck to their values and that is what has helped make them successful – Boudicca, Martin Luther King, Thomas Paine, Florence Nightingale, Mahatma Ghandi, Nelson Mandela and Anita Roddick, for example.

CHAPTER 7

Discovering your strengths

Do you remember when you got something wrong at school and had do it again and again and again until you got it right? My personal purgatory was spelling. It always has been, even at university. Finally my dean sent me off to an educational psychologist who, after several tests, was very flattering about my IQ but derogatory about my spelling, reporting to the dean that I had a spelling age of a 13-year-old. Not much has changed during my career and I must have ruined the spelling of at least three PAs.

Repeating all of those spelling lists again and again was like pushing a rock up a mountain: impossible! 'Impossible' was reputed not to be a word in Napoleon Bonaparte's 'dictionary' but, as far as spelling goes, it is in mine. Why all this personal disclosure? Because in life more attention is given to our inadequacies, blind spots, hiccups, boo-boos, opportunities, challenges and a legion of other disguises which all stand for weaknesses and/or errors.

The word 'criticism' originated from the Greek (κριτης) meaning judgement of whether something is right or wrong, with the emphasis often on the latter. Sadly, all too often there is a strong cultural proclivity to find what is wrong in something or someone rather than finding what is right and discovering their strengths. We also have a temptation to give up on something because we accept our own limitations and say to ourselves 'I can't do that because I'm ...'

'Argue for your limitations and sure enough they are yours.'

Richard Bach, author of *Jonathan Livingston Seagull*

During the latter part of the last century there was a huge emphasis, mainly in America, on being a 'winner'. This was hammered home by fire-and-brimstone motivational speakers preaching the mantra that it was possible to achieve whatever you wanted, all you had to do was to be highly motivated, totally committed, work on it 24/7 and overcome every obstacle no matter what. Such erroneous preaching did more harm than good.

Thankfully sanity has returned now it has been realised that hard work, commitment, etc. is no match for raw talent plus hard work. We've also realised that it's not possible to achieve everything you want, and nor should it be. We can, however, achieve far more when we concentrate on our strengths, talents and competences. Here are some famous examples:

● Richard Branson as a teenager was selling budgerigars that he had bred and Christmas trees. At the age of 20 he was selling mail-order records, at 22 he built a recording studio and at 27 headed the sixth largest record company in the world. This was achieved through entrepreneurial talent and effort which has continued throughout his life and resulted in a billion-dollar fortune. I'm sure there were many contemporaries of Sir Richard at Stowe School, just as clever, just as hard working, but, without that entrepreneurial talent, they were unlikely to have done quite so well.

● Philip Green shares a similar story. He started in retail at 15, pulled off a fantastic deal at 22 importing jeans, then, with friends, bought a company for a song that was £30 million in debt to be sold within three years for £550

million. I am sure there were many just as clever, just
as hard-working contemporaries of Sir Philip at Carmel
College, but, without that entrepreneurial talent ...

brilliant example

When the verger of St Martin's Church retired, Tom, who worked in the
village newsagents, asked the vicar if he could be considered for the
position, only to be told that, as he couldn't read or write, he couldn't be
an applicant.

Although Tom could not read or write, he was very popular and exceptional
at sales. Some years later, Tom had saved enough to buy a little shop of
his own. He was so successful that he bought the newsagents where he
originally worked. That too went well. Before long, through continual hard
work and his retail skills, and some significant acquisitions, Tom became a
very successful retailer with a national chain of shops.

Tom was a real benefactor of children's charities both here and abroad.
His generosity was so well known that he was invited to be interviewed
by Michael Parkinson. About halfway through the interview Parkie asked
Tom, 'Now is there anything unusual about you that we don't know?' Tom
sheepishly replied, 'Well actually I can't read or write.'

'What,' said Parkie 'a retail legend such as yourself cannot read or write?!'
Just think what you could have done if you could read or write!' 'Yes,'
replied Tom humbly, 'I would have been the verger of St Martins.'

Many people work hard, but not to their strengths.

Assessing your strengths

The following activity takes courage!

 activity

Look at the list below and select the 10 attributes that reflect your strengths. Then rank them in terms of importance. This is the easy part. Then give the list to someone who knows you well and whose views you respect and ask them to select and rank these items as if they were you!

Accepting	Courteousness	Grace
Acumen	Creativity	Gregariousness
Adaptability	Dedication	Hard working
Ambition	Determination	Humility
Astuteness	Diplomacy	Humour
Authenticity	Discretion	Ideals
Balanced	Drive	Imaginative
Brave	Empathy	Independence
Bright	Endurance	Individuality
Buoyant	Energy	Influence
Calmness	Enthusiasm	Insight
Charisma	Expressivity	Integrity
Charm	Faithfulness	Intelligence
Consciousness	Flexibility	Knowledgeable
Cheerfulness	Genuineness	Leadership
Commitment	Good fortune	Loyalty
Confidence	Good judgement	Maturity
Compassion	Goal orientation	Modesty
Conscientious	Good social skills	Objectivity
Courage	Generosity	Opportunism

Optimism	Reliability	Style
Originality	Responsible	Understanding
Patience	Self-control	Verve
Passion	Serenity	Vibrancy
Poise	Self-confidence	Vision
Principled	Self-discipline	Vitality
Proactive	Selflessness	Warmness
Prudence	Sincerity	Willpower
Realistic	Sophistication	Wisdom
Resilience	Spirituality	Zeal

I am confident that I have and can demonstrate to the world the following strengths, in rank order, with my dominant strength first:

1st _____

2nd _____

3rd _____

4th _____

5th _____

6th _____

7th _____

8th _____

9th _____

10th _____

Next, against each strength above, provide an example of an achievement – as recent as possible – that would justify your claim that you have this strength/talent.

Now it's your friend's turn.

My confidant/colleague/friend thinks that I have and demonstrate to the world:

1st _____

2nd _____

3rd _____

4th _____

5th _____

6th _____

7th _____

8th _____

9th _____

10th _____

Now comes the fun feedback part. Discuss any similarities/differences between your views about yourself and those of your confidant/colleague/ friend.

Let's see how realistic you have been in making an assessment of yourself:

● What has been confirmed?

● What has taken you by surprise?

● How might any differences have come about?

● Should you/could you do anything about the differences?

● How has this activity improved your understanding of yourself?

Now do some work on the major question: **how will you play to your strengths in the future?**

Strengths from the animal kingdom

Here is another somewhat frivolous activity which is both fun and revealing.

 **activity**

With your partner or a longstanding friend who knows you well, choose an animal (bird, reptile, fish, insect or mammal) that you think could represent you. Your partner or friend does the same, again as if they were you.

List down adjectives that your animal represents, for example:

- Dog: faithful, friendly, positive, persistent, intelligent, inquisitive, etc.
- Eagle: powerful, flies above things, top of the food chain, individual rather than one of a flock, etc.
- Dolphin: intelligent, fun, friendly, fast, etc.
- Domestic cat: independent, curious, playful, can fall asleep anywhere and any time, does not have a master but has servants
- Owl: wise, mature, reflective.

Now the fun starts. See if your partner/friend has the same animal and what adjectives they would ascribe to their choice.

 'When restraint and courtesy are added to strength, the latter becomes irresistible.'

Mahatma Gandhi, civil rights leader and politician

 'Only one who devotes himself to a cause with his whole strength can be a true master.'

Albert Einstein

And to show that I cannot be serious all the time:

'Youngsters of the age of two and three are endowed with extraordinary strength. They can lift a dog twice their own weight and dump him into the bath.'

Erma Bombeck, American humourist

brilliant recap

- The purpose of the activities in this chapter has been to encourage you to identify your strengths so you can play to them as much as possible. No one can be good at everything.

- Consider this: what is common in the following famous people – Agatha Christie, Hans Christian Andersen, and two of my favourite people, Richard Branson and Leonardo di ser Piero da Vinci? Answer: strangely enough they were, or are all, dyslexics who played to their strengths. I wonder what would have happened if they had to take an English exam as an entrance qualification for their profession.

CHAPTER 8

Developing your vision

The idea of developing a personal vision for ourselves is a relatively recent luxury. Self-help books emerged in the 1950s and have been prolific ever since. Their birth coincided with the arrival of increased leisure time allowing people to ponder their lot – particularly those who experienced the death and deprivation of two world wars. This fashion for 'vision' has also been taken up by the corporate world – so if they are spending time and money on this important aspect of development then so should we.

During the 1950s, people began to ask 'What is it all about?' and 'Where am I in all this?' Then came questions such as 'What do I want?' (notice that it was not 'What do I need?') and 'How do I get it?' The culture of deprivation had changed; gone were the days of Henry Ford's famous saying 'You can have any colour you want providing it's black', and at the end of the 1950s the question became 'What colour would you like?'

This was accelerated by the dilution of a class system: now your background was no deterrent to your education or success in a career. Such aspirants naturally began to ask 'How do I get to the top?' Having a personal vision is critical to achieve the elixir of success. Not having a vision blinds you to seeing life's opportunities – except in retrospect.

The simplest definition of a personal vision is a statement of intent for your life. But that belies its power. Having a vision gives meaning to your life. A vision answers the 'What's it all about?' question. It provides a wonderful opportunity to be your true self and know where you want to go. Whatever your circumstances your personal vision will, quite literally, allow you to see your way through life.

brilliant example

Here is one of the most compelling personal vision statements:

Let the first act of every morning be to make the following resolve for the day:

- I shall not fear anyone on Earth.
- I shall fear only God.
- I shall not bear ill-will toward anyone.
- I shall not submit to injustice from anyone.
- I shall conquer untruth by truth.
- And in resisting untruth, I shall put up with all suffering.

Mahatma Gandhi

Creating a personal vision will require you to do some serious thinking about the future: what you want to be and what you want to get out of your brief sojourn on earth. But, without one, it's easy to drift through life on autopilot.

Even worse, some people choose to wear blinkers and simply not think about where they are going or how to extract themselves from situations they are not happy with. Better the devil you know? Surely not. These people will one day realise that they have become fully paid-up members of the 'should have' tribe with far too many regrets in their past.

Any journey made out of ignorance can't be very helpful. Without the benefit of a vision to guide and validate our lives 'there' ends up looking and feeling like the 'here' where we began. And flying blind into new situations can lead to wrong turns and missed opportunities. By reading this text you have put yourself on the road to a more purposeful life. And the work you have done up until now will have helped you gain a deeper understanding of who you are, your strengths, your weaknesses, your values, skills and competences because all of these have a direct effect on our vision.

The better we know ourselves and what we want, the more powerful and appropriate our vision will be. Interestingly, because you have done this work on yourself, your vision has probably already begun to emerge and claim you.

The problems of doing

For many people, life is filled with more and more 'doing'. We work, shop, sleep, cook, eat, clean, travel and entertain ourselves, and so our hours are filled with completing tasks or activities.

One frightening statistic, according to Nielson's People Meter, is that the majority of us watch 18 hours of television per week, which is 936 hours per year or 39 days of continuous watching each year.

The danger is that if all of this doing is unfocused and not guided by an overriding vision, you will find yourself stuck in the same situation because none of your 'doing' has been helping you get going. In other words, if you want to get out of an existence of 'doing' then a 'vision' or 'purpose' is essential.

'Ever more people today have the means to live, but no meaning to live for.'

Viktor Frankl, author of *Man's Search for Meaning* (written after his survival from Auschwitz)[1]

Health warning

You may find that having a vision and pursuing it will make you significantly different from others – and you may find, like the following people, that you need to break through social norms to realise your vision:

- Jesus broke the rules of Judaism.
- Columbus broke the rules of navigation.
- Nelson broke the rules of naval engagement.
- Darwin broke the rules of creationism.
- Gandhi broke the rules of resistance.
- Ford broke the rules of manufacturing.
- Joyce broke the rules of writing.
- Presley broke the rules of popular music.
- Branson is still breaking the rules of almost everything he touches.

 **brilliant** activity

Developing a vision

For each question tick the appropriate box. This isn't a very complicated activity but your responses will give you all the answers you need about the

---

1 Frankl's book is the most wonderful endorsement for the need for a personal vision. If you ever doubt that life has meaning then read this life-affirming book.

strength of your vision – if you have one at all – and how powerfully you are using it.

1 Do you have a vision in your life?

Yes ☐   Possibly ☐ ·   No ☐

2 Do you make your 'life decisions' according to the vision you have?

Yes ☐   Possibly ☐   No ☐

3 Do you monitor on a regular basis how you are working to your vision?

Yes ☐   Possibly ☐   No ☐

4 Do you research options that will assist you to achieve your vision?

Yes ☐   Possibly ☐   No ☐

5 Do you spend regular time reviewing your vision to see if it is still valid for you?

Yes ☐   Possibly ☐   No ☐

6 Do you have your vision written down?

Yes ☐   Possibly ☐   No ☐

7 Do you discuss your vision with your partner?

Yes ☐   Possibly ☐   No ☐

8 Do you actively discard those things that don't help you achieve your vision?

Yes ☐   Possibly ☐   No ☐

9 Do you have a life that is in balance?

Yes ☐   Possibly ☐   No ☐

10 Do you reward yourself when you achieve things that are in line with your vision?

Yes ☐   Possibly ☐   No ☐

For self-development, having a vision for yourself is very important. Scoring here is very simple: if you have five or more 'No's' then the advice is to seriously consider developing a vision for yourself.

 'Where there is no vision, the people perish.'

Proverbs 29:18

Creating a personal vision

The purpose of having a personal vision is for you to maximise the return on your effort to date and to maximise the yield on the mental, emotional, physical and spiritual outlay you have invested in your life and career to date.

In developing your vision, this is where your work, so far, begins to come together. Having decided to take charge of your life, a vision for yourself becomes paramount. If you don't have a vision for yourself, your future will just bob around on the sea of life. Not only that, your life will be highly influenced by what other people want of you. The best vision statements are those that describe you as you will be in 5–10 years' time, possibly even further.

Spend time asking yourself the important question: **what is my preferred future?**

To do this:

● Review and reflect on your previous achievements, skills and competences, and your beliefs.
● Describe what you want to be in the future:
  – be as specific as you can
  – be optimistic and inspiring.

Your vision should be exciting and motivating.

Spend extra time reviewing your value system.

- Which values are key for you?
- Which should be reflected in your vision statement?
- How in the future will your key values be obvious to all?

Creating a vision statement

Once you have done this preliminary work you are ready to define your vision statement, which is both a statement of purpose and of function. Your vision statement should:

- reflect all the information that you have discovered about yourself
- reflect yourself in the future as if you have achieved it and you are already there (It's as if you already exist in the future state.)
- be as exact as possible and not expressed in generalisations
- be realistic
- besides being aspirational and inspirational, your vision must also be measurable
- make you proud and excited
- be as short as possible.

Here I'd like to share my personal vision statement to give you a concrete example of what a vision statement looks like. My statement was written in the mid-1980s when I went through the trauma of being fired and I promised myself never to work within an organisation again:

I am happily married with children who respect and love me, running my own business in an HR related field and leveraging off my psychology knowledge, corporate experience and people skills in a successful consultancy. I am an established international author with several best sellers to my name. I am an Anglican priest who is known for his compassion, meaningful sermons and teaching skills.

Benefits of visioning

Visioning:

- takes you out of your day-to-day thinking and insists that you are future orientated
- helps you make the appropriate significant decisions for yourself
- provides continuity and predictability
- identifies direction and purpose
- tells others where you are going
- promotes laser-like focus
- encourages openness to unique and creative solutions
- builds self-confidence.

Vision assassins

As you engage in the visioning process, be alert to the following vision assassins:

- fear of losing friends[2]
- fear of ridicule[3]
- complacency and procrastination
- short-term thinking.

---

2 All your friends will want you to be successful but not more successful than they are.

3 It was held that:
  - the four-minute mile was impossible;
  - national interest would prevent the Common Market;
  - there would not be a man on the moon during the 20th century; and
  - computers could only be afforded by big organisations.

 **brilliant** recap

- A personal vision is essential if you are going to steer your life and career.

- Your vision should be based in reality but with a great deal of 'stretch' in it.

- Your vision must be motivational.

- Your vision must be written in the present tense.

- For success, you must be committed to your vision.

CHAPTER 9

Developing
your mission

Sometimes there is confusion between vision and mission, but they serve a complementary purpose. When we unpack the word 'mission' it will help us to understand the difference between the two.

definition

Mission

A predetermined course of action or a combination of assignments to help accomplish your vision of yourself. Mission is a strange idea, having its roots as a religious activity. There are two main concepts which underlie it: first an objective, such as a place or state of being, and secondly movement towards that place or state.

So a vision is the 'what' you want to achieve and the mission is the 'how'. In other words, now you know what your vision is, you need to work out how you are going to achieve it; vision is the end point and mission is the map for the journey.

If your vision is to be achieved then you have to be psychologically and emotionally fully committed to it, otherwise you are more than likely to fail.

Examples of commitment

Thomas Edison, who invented the light bulb, tested over 6000 materials before he discovered how to coat the thin platinum filament in the glass vacuum bulb, which would delay the filament from melting after a few hours.

John F. Kennedy had a mission – to put a man on the moon. It took years of research, billions of dollars, total effort from the whole team and huge courage on the part of the astronauts. The path to success would not have been easy, but the level of commitment propelled them to success.

 **example**

How to turn a vision into a mission

The vision: to be a good family man, a devout Christian who is recognised for his wisdom and understanding. I will be a successful retail professional in all respects so that I can provide for my family needs and be able financially to assist those worse off than myself, particularly the disabled.

This vision translates into the specifics of a mission in the following ways:

1 **Good family man**. Keeping the spirit of my marriage vows and ensuring love, respect and quality time for my wife and my children. Providing the best standard of living that I can and setting up trusts for my children.

2 **Devout Christian**. Attending church regularly, participating wherever I can with the talents that I have and keeping the golden rule.

3 **Wisdom and understanding**. Developing myself, reading regularly, keeping up with current affairs, offering myself as a mentor and tutoring my children and their friends.

4 **Successful retailer**. Learning all aspects of the trade, developing a reputation as being fair in all dealing and maximising customer service.

5 **Assisting the disabled**. Making regular charitable donations; undertaking charity and volunteer work; and initiating and participating in fund-raising events.

 **tip**

'To ensure that your work is also play, I recommend that you develop a personal mission statement. This will help you find out what it is you enjoy so much that you lose track of time when you're doing it.'

Ken Blanchard, author of the *One Minute Manager*

Pushing yourself

Back to where we started: 'If it's going to be, then it's down to me.' Now if this is to be achieved then you have to be proactive – it's up to you to push the boundaries and push yourself.

 **activity**

Use your heroes to help you develop your mission

If you could be anyone in the world who would you be? You can choose from history, literature, films, politics, religion – anyone at all – even change your gender if you wish to. You can choose up to three people.

1 _____

2 _____

3 _____

Why have you chosen these people? Reflect on these three people who are significant for you. What might their personal mission have been? What did they actually do to achieve their vision? (What they did and how they did it reveals their mission.)

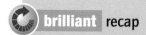 recap

- You need a mission for your vision to be achieved. Your mission details how you need to behave in order to achieve your vision.

- To achieve your mission takes personal effort, persistence and psychological strength to cope with setbacks.

CHAPTER 10

Developing and achieving your goals

ow we have our vision and our mission, we need to put some flesh on our broad mission objective. Being specific and realistic are the keys to success as we move from overarching statements to definite pragmatism. Let's begin looking at developing possible goals.

Goals have to be specific, which means something quantifiable. If you can't measure it, handle it or qualify it then it is not an effective goal. Saying something like: 'I want to be good/happy/rich/spiritual' is about as useful as going into a greengrocers and telling the assistant 'I want to buy some fruit.' It would be more helpful, but only just, if you said 'I would like some stone fruit.' Even better still would be 'I want to buy three peaches and a pound of plums.'

Fat versus thin words

The more thin (precise) you can be with a goal the better.

For example:

I want a companion animal.

   Pet is better than animal,

      Dog is better than pet,

         Terrier is better than dog,

            Jack Russell is better than terrier.

This will make sure that you do not end up with an Eclectus parrot or an Utsurimono koi; both can however make great companions.

We call words which cover a class of something such as family, pets, tools, vehicles, etc., 'fat' words and they are just not helpful. Fat words do have their place. Politicians are great at these sorts of words as part of their regular sound bites. They want 'the best for the country and the future', which means being efficient with resources and ensuring that we have a labour force which has the skills, guided by effective senior management with the vision to ensure that our children and our children's children, not forgetting the aged, etc., etc. All said with a resounding 'here, here' from the backbench supporters of all hues. Why? Because from this plethora of fat words each person will have their own interpretation of what is being said, adding the specifics of their own preferential choosing. Everyone would agree that to be successful you must get back to basics; the problem is whose basics?

Realistic means just what it says – it has to be possible. For example Khagendra Thapa Magar from Nepal who stands just 65.5 cm tall cannot, as the smallest man in the world, however hard he tries or no matter how much time he puts in, achieve a goal of being like my friend Jesse White (an Australian AFL athlete) who stands a perfectly proportioned man at 197 cm. Let alone Ajaz Ahmed, the world's tallest living person at the time of writing, who is a meagre 254 cms.

SMARTI goals

As you write out your goals you will find that you become committed to them. You might have a great memory as far as your goals are concerned but the contingencies of everyday life have a way of ensuring that they are easily overlooked. When you write your goal employing the SMARTI format detailed below, there can be no doubt about whether or not you have achieved that goal.

- **S = Specific**
- **M = Measurable**

- **A = Achievable**
- **R = Realistic/Relevant**
- **T = Time-bound**
- **I = Interesting**

Specific

Goals have to be specific which means something quantifiable. If you cannot measure it, handle it or qualify it then it is not an effective goal. Saying something like: 'I want to be good/happy/ rich/spiritual' is about as useful as, as we have shown, going into a travel agent and saying you want a holiday.

Measurable

A goal that cannot be quantified in terms of money, percentages, length or breadth, weight or time is not a goal. For example, 'I will spend more time with my partner' or 'I will lose weight' are not goals. However, 'My partner and I will have at least one "date night" once a month' and 'I will lose 5 kilos' are goals because you can measure whether you have achieved them or not.

Achievable

All goals should have some 'stretch' in them: achievable with effort; just out of reach at present but not out of sight. For example, I will lose '5 kilos in two weeks' is just not possible without radical surgery.

Realistic

Realistic means just what it says – it has to be possible.

Time-bound

Again this means what it says – within a specific time period. Yes, you could lose 5 kilos but by when? To lose 5 kilos in six months is achievable, measurable, possible and time-bound.

Interesting

This is necessary motivation. If the goal is of no real interest to you or just done under obligation you will probably suffer from procrastination and/or lack of commitment.

Four types of goal behaviour

Interestingly, there are basically four types of goal behaviour, but only one of them is anywhere near successful in goal achievement. It's the one that implements the following formula:

$$Energy + Focus = Commitment$$

Energy here is not about being busy; it's easy to be busy but not effective. It's about powering forward. Focus is not about seeing everything perfectly but seeing everything that matters perfectly.

These two essential forces combine to make commitment or action. That commitment gives you the discipline not to be swayed by distractions, and to overcome slippage and setbacks. It also warns you when any of those impulses tempt you to digress from the main game, keeping you on the fast track to achieving your goals.

The four types of goal behaviour are:

The postponer

We start with the worst. Each year the postponer wins the 'Round to it Award', because when they get close to the crucial action they somehow never quite get 'round to it'. Their pontificating on what they are going to do is worthy of a Roman orator. They will remind you of the truism 'when all is said and done, more is always said than done'. Some fear failure so never take the first step from the base camp to the mountain called Achievement.

The muddled

For this person so many things are going on all at once. They are so busy putting out little fires that they do not notice the next fire starting up, or put in place fire prevention strategies. As someone once said, 'It's difficult to remember that you are draining the lake when you are up to your bottom in alligators!' These people are energetic and they work hard and with enthusiasm just like the rodent on a treadmill – going fast, going in circles, going nowhere.

The loner

This person suffers from goal hyperopia; they are so close to the action but their eyesight is blurred. They can see the big picture and describe it perfectly, but can't do anything about it. Loners know they need the honey but just stare at the flowers.

The doers

These are the people that have the right concoction of focus and energy, the elixir of achievement, combining focus and energy, demolishing uncertainty and roadblocks. They are on track, on time and onto success.

The goal behaviour matrix

On the next page is a diagram which illustrates how these elements are combined.

Reflect on a couple of goals that you have set yourself in the past which you have not achieved. Do you place yourself in one of the boxes 1 to 3 on the diagram? This is not to shame you, but so that you can understand whether in future you should concentrate on improving either your energy or your focus, guaranteeing that your current goals will not be frustrated.

Nature is not fair in her distribution of gifts. Some of you will naturally have more energy, and others better powers of focus

		Low	High
Focus	High	Loner 1	Doer 4
	Low	Postponer 2	Muddler 3

Low · High

Energy level

and attention, but everyone can advance and improve on the gifts that they are naturally given.

Setting milestones

On your journey towards your goal, set predetermined milestones along the way. These landmarks can be thought of as sub-parts of the final goal which need to be achieved in sequence. A simple example would be where the goal is to build a house and the milestones would be completing the foundations, then the walls and then the roof. On the completion of each milestone, reward yourself.

Setting rewards

What is interesting about rewards is that they actually increase your commitment and your motivation. To keep yourself motivated, celebrate when you have achieved a milestone. Revel in the satisfaction of having reached your sub-goal. One way to do this is to develop a reward schedule for yourself, your family or friends to measure everyone's progress and celebrate together.

brilliant tips

1   Break each goal down into milestones along the way and give yourself a small reward each and every time you pass a milestone. Rewards could be, for example, a bottle of your favourite wine or a trip to the cinema.

2   When you achieve your goal a big self-reward is justified. We remember the big reward just as much as we do the actual achievement. Enjoy large rewards for big achievements: buying some clothing or jewellery, taking your partner away for the weekend, or treating yourself to a holiday.

3   Your rewards should be highly personal. We are all motivated by different things so select something that will make your heart sing and keep your motivation high for the next goal.

4   Remember, as you reward yourself let your 'inner voice' say 'I am doing this because I have just ...' so that you connect your behaviour with the reward. This fulfils the psychological maxim 'what gets positively rewarded leads to repeated positive behaviour'.

Setting goal priorities

brilliant activity

Take the following list, presented alphabetically, and re-order the items, ranking them according to your life so far to construct your list of near-term priorities. Don't group together or merge any of the items.

Career	Current income
Children	Equity ownership
Co-workers	Family and significant others
Contribution to society	Financial security

Friends	Personal growth
Geographical location	Prestige and status
Health and fitness	Professional growth
Influence and power	Relationships
Intrinsic nature of work	Relocation
Leisure time	Retirement
Life balance	Security
Personal challenge	Spiritual wellbeing
Personal finances	Work environment

Other (please specify) _____

My top five goal priorities at this time are:

1 _____

2 _____

3 _____

4 _____

5 _____

Understanding your priorities gives you a concrete tool for evaluating your life options. It helps you decide which are most important for you and how you should allocate your time, effort and investment to achieve the goal.

 **brilliant** activity

Personal goals (short- and long-term)

Take the five goal priorities you have written above and set them out on a sheet of A4 paper.

Under each of the priorities write three SMARTI goals. The more SMARTI you make your goals as you write them, the more tangible they become. Written words tend to become fixed in our minds, which is why it's good to commit them to paper – another reason for keeping a log book.

Your short-term goals should dovetail and support your long-term goals. Obvious but true: if you know where you are going you are more likely to get there. Also, having long-term goals gives your life structure. In my consultancy practice we have worked with many executives who, at the age of 50, have found themselves in an organisational cul-de-sac. When asked why they took their last job, many reply, 'Because it was offered to me'. They did not ask themselves, 'How does this fit into my five-year plan?' with the result that they are stuck and unable to move forward.

Of course you can review your goals, amending them if necessary or as and when your situation changes. It is impossible to predict what will happen in the future but having a plan is better than drifting. At the end of the year you might like to reassess the categories based on any changes in your experience and situation.

Short-term goals

My short-term goals (possible within one year)

Family and significant others:

1 _____

2 _____

3 _____

▶

Health and fitness

1 _____

2 _____

3 _____

Professional growth

1 _____

2 _____

3 _____

Financial security

1 _____

2 _____

3 _____

Career

1 _____

2 _____

3 _____

Life balance

1 _____

2 _____

3 _____

Long-term goals

Short-term goals are rather like a springboard to help you to achieve in the future. For instance, to be the CFO of a significant organisation with a turnover of €100 million, you need to achieve your short-term goals such as a professional qualification and perhaps an MBA and do the hard yards of working and moving up the hierarchy (project manager to management accountant to financial analyst to group accountant) to get to CFO. The next jump could be to CEO. (Off the topic but some valuable career advice: If you are ambitious then apply the 'get, gobble and go' strategy. Don't stay in a job to enjoy the successes you've achieved but use those successes as leverage to the next appropriate promotion. In this way you move so fast that your failures do not catch up with you!)

My long-term goals (possible within five years)

Family and significant others:

1 _____
2 _____
3 _____

Health and fitness

1 _____
2 _____
3 _____

Professional growth

1 _____
2 _____
3 _____

Financial security

1 _____
2 _____
3 _____

Career

1 _____
2 _____
3 _____

▶

Life balance

1 _____

2 _____

3 _____

To give you a 'reality' check discuss your short- and long-term goals with your partner and with someone whose opinion you trust – a family member, best friend, mentor, coach, etc.

 'The greatest danger in life for most of us is not that our aim is too high and we miss it, but that it is too low and we reach it.'

Michelangelo Buonarroti

 'Only those who risk going too far can possibly find out how far one can go.'

T.S. Eliot, poet

Planning your route

You have now gained a thorough understanding of yourself and undertaken a rigorous fitness regime for self-development, including setting your short- and long-term goals. You have all the tools you need to get going. But do you know where you are going?

It is trite but right: 'If you fail to plan then you plan to fail.' It's of no use knowing what you want and where you want to go unless you have a plan. A map for the journey is essential. Not having a plan reminds me of two people heading down the motorway at top speed and one saying to the other, 'Where are we going?', only to get the reply, 'Who cares – we are making great time'.

Having a plan will:

- give you greater focus on your chosen destination and what exactly you want to achieve
- enable you to set the benchmark or standard that you wish to achieve
- help you anticipate potential difficulties and how you might overcome them
- ensure you have the resources you need
- gather the advice you need.

The benefits of planning

Planning will:

- help you visualise the promise of the future by cutting through clutter
- enable you to co-ordinate effort
- allow you to iron out the wrinkles in your goal
- help you to size up your performance and measure your progress
- enable you to put contingencies in place
- give you the tools you need to deal with sudden and unexpected problems
- reveal roadblocks
- give you a clear picture of how different tasks and activities interact to ensure success
- stimulate your thinking
- lead you onward and upward by providing the stimulation you need to avoid dead-ends and blind alleys
- act as a catalyst for new insights and ideas
- offer an exit plan
- give you a sneak preview of what is expected and allow you to judge for yourself if the investment is worth the risk

- serve as an early warning system, allowing you to bow out gracefully rather than be thrown out later on
- save you a long time in regret and misery.

The benefits of planning sound almost too good to be true. But, this time, the hype is legitimate. Planning is everything it's cut out to be. Perfect the use of planning and you will win many battles by default.

Having a plan in your head is not as effective as having a written plan. In the latter you will find that your thoughts develop a life of their own and become a potential reality, a springboard for action. Have you ever gone shopping knowing everything you want and returned home only to realise that you have forgotten something crucial as well as being a victim of the impulse purchase?[1] Your simple shopping list – the plan – saves you both time and money.

A plan helps you make a commitment to yourself, pointing you towards the future. You also know when you have scored a personal development goal.

If your mind is like mine then you will pay more attention to today's contingencies. What I should be doing for tomorrow somehow slips into the oblivion of the now, only to surface later, accompanied by its good friend regret, to beat me up.

You can virtually guarantee your success in any endeavour if you know who you are, what you want, where you are going, how you will get there, and what you will do once you arrive. Planning before you act helps you to do things better, faster and cheaper! Planning offers a host of other tasty benefits as well.

1 According to the American Bureau of Statistics, in some retail categories as much as 60% of sales can be attributed to impulse purchasing.

Making a plan

If your goals are in a SMARTI format you have almost developed your plan. However, goals will not be achieved unless there is action and actions need a plan.

Here are the major steps:

1 Read your vision, your mission statements and your goal category (e.g. health and wellbeing).

2 Take the 'S' from your SMARTI goal and make it the heading for your plan sheet.

3 Through research make a list of the things you will need to accomplish the goal.

4 The 'T' from your SMARTI goal will give you the end date by which you will achieve your goal. However, set a date for the accomplishment of all the sub-goals (e.g. acquiring each resource you will need). If you need training then you need to establish by when, otherwise the project will stall.

5 List all the actions that you will have to take.

6 Review what help, advice or assistance you might need and secure it.

7 Think through what difficulties might arise and develop contingency plans.

8 Once a month, or more if necessary, re-evaluate where you are and reschedule if required.

9 Reward yourself and those involved.

 **recap**

- Goals need to be specific, measurable, achievable, realistic, time-bound and interesting in order for you to use them effectively.

- Combine 'doer' goal behaviour with the formula: Energy + Focus = Commitment, for success.

- Remember to reward yourself for small successes, as well as the bigger ones, along the way.

- Set goal priorities and long- and short-term goals to give you an unshakable goal structure.

- Create a plan of action.

CHAPTER 11

Developing your motivation

Motivation is not an easy concept. There are so many opinions and theories about motivation that it appears difficult to pin down. In fact, it's rather like a seahorse – you know what it looks like but could you describe it to a friend so that they could draw it accurately?

Here is a romp through motivation theory in one long sentence (of 80 words):

We all want air, safety, friends, status and to be the best (Maslow), when someone discovers our hot buttons and uses them (Pavlov and Skinner) especially if it is an opportunity to grow (Hertzberg) or if we expect to be rewarded, and there is a real chance of getting it if we do something, then there is a high probability that we will do that something (Lawler and Vroom): however, our behaviour reflects what we think is equitable (Stacey Adams).

See what I mean about the seahorse? Trying to describe everyone's thoughts on motivation in one place ends up muddled and confused. So let's try to clarify things within the remit of self-development.

What motivates you?

We need to understand what specifically motivates you. Here we turn to a brilliant Harvard psychologist, David McClelland, who suggested that each of us have three fundamental needs, but that one would be more dominant than the other two. Our three basic motivational needs are as follows.

Need for power

Some people just love to be in control. It doesn't matter what they are doing, they are most comfortable in themselves when they have the role of leader. People with this need enjoy and will work to gain power and influence. Their jellybean is to be able to persuade others to their way of thinking and doing. Such people assume control whenever they can and they have interests and seek positions which will satisfy their need for power. These people make a rush to the top of organisations and not infrequently they have shadows of megalomania and narcissism.

Need for affiliation

Other people just love being interactive with others, networking, making new friends and maintaining friendships. A sense of belonging within a social set(s) is very important to them. For such people, being popular and being liked is high on the agenda. They will work hard to achieve affiliation with others both during their leisure time and in their careers. At social gatherings, such individuals do their very best to ensure that everyone is interacting and having an enjoyable time. They are the host with the most or the hostess with the mostest. When the need for affiliation dominates the individual there is a danger of suffering from the 'disease to please'.

Need for achievement

It is not the rewards of success that motivate the people with a need for achievement, but the journey itself and getting to the goal that they have set themselves. Individuals in this category are not usually highly competitive because they gain satisfaction from the doing rather than the recognition or the status that the achievement will bring. Money, status and/or praise do not count for much; it's the satisfaction in the job itself and seeing the result that is of prime importance. It's the effort more than the arrival that brings satisfaction. Being stretched to achieve greater things is the jellybean here. Constant feedback on their progress is a requirement because such people need to know how they stand and how well they have been doing.

What is your need?

Complete the activity below. With a little reflection it should not be too difficult for you to identify which category you feel most comfortable in. Remember that we all have needs to do with power, affiliation and achievement, but usually one is more important and preferable to the others.

Knowing what your preference is will help you to understand and accept why others do not get as excited about the things that you do. It's not that they are not motivated, it's just that they have a different motivational need embedded within their personality.

 **activity**

What motivates you?

Most people, once they have satisfied their basic and social needs, are motivated by three major needs: for personal significance, to be empowered and to be challenged. Below are examples of each category. Whilst we are motivated by elements in all three, which category do you find reflects you the most?

Significance/Affiliation:

- I want to be liked/popular.
- I want to do meaningful work.
- I want to contribute.
- I want to be respected.
- I want to make a difference.
- I want to be known for my expertise.
- I want to be admired for who I am.

▶

Empowerment/Power:

- I want to be autonomous.
- I want freedom to choose.
- I want to make decisions.
- I want to be accountable.
- I want to be my own person.
- I want personal authority.
- I want to set my own rules.

Challenge/Achievement:

- I want to develop myself.
- I want to use all my competences.
- I want to take risks.
- I want to learn new skills.
- I want to be the best I can.
- I want increased responsibility.
- I want to compete with myself.

It would appear that of the three, my main motivation is:

_____

If it was easy for you to decide which category reflected your style then it might be worth considering, in terms of personal development, nurturing the other two. Being like a three-legged stool you would then be stable anywhere and be successful in most situations.

brilliant tip

If your motivation fails and you come to a standstill, don't beat yourself up, give yourself a rest. When you are ready, look back and see how far you have come and reflect on your achievements to date, and the time, effort and cost that you have already invested in this goal and your vision. This should be sufficient to encourage you to start again.

'Motivation is a fire within. If someone else tries to light that fire underneath you, chances are it will burn very briefly.'

Stephen Covey, self-development guru

When your motivation flags

And it will, because the old 'you' is very seductive at whispering in your ear, 'This is too hard, let's go back to the way you used to be'. So try the following:

● If you are a 'significance' person say to yourself: 'If I want to make a difference, be respected and make an impact it is essential I do this.'

● If you are an 'empowerment' person say to yourself: 'If I want to be accountable, autonomous and be my own person then it is essential I do this.'

● If you are a 'challenge' person say to yourself: 'If I want be competent, develop new skills and be the very best I can it is essential I do this.'

● Develop an appropriate mantra based on the above and say it to yourself on a daily basis at least twice a day. It's no good thinking it or even reading it. For it to be effective it must be said with determination and as loudly as possible so you drive it into your subconscious. In Australia we are fortunate because no one is more than two hours from either bush, wilderness or desert – perfect places to really shout your mantra again and again until the words begin to lose their meaning. You will feel strange at first, perhaps even silly, but just observe how your subsequent behaviour slowly changes.

Use your log book

As we know, 'past behaviour is the best indicator of future behaviour' and if you can accomplish something once you can do it again. Your log book provides great support as you re-read all your achievements. This provokes the idea: 'If I had not done XXX then I would not have achieved YYY' which leads to 'Well if I want YYY2 then I must get on and do XXX2'.

 activity

Reflection and self-talk for when demotivation strikes

In a quiet moment spend some time in reflection and ask yourself:

- Have I been too enthusiastic and set my objective too high? Should I reduce it to something more achievable?
- Am I working too hard at my objective and am I exhausting myself?
- Should I be more gentle with myself?
- When did I feel demotivated like this before?
- How did I cope then?
- How long did it last?
- Should I give myself a rest for the same amount of time?
- Could I work on another area of my plan and return to this later?
- What did I do to re-motivate myself?
- Can I do that now?
- Who helped me get back on track?
- How quickly can I contact them?

A little poem:

This is very personal. It's a little poem that I say to myself during periods of downtime and it goes something like this:

'He who fights and runs away,
Lives to fight another day.'

Now what's interesting about these 11 words is that the person is not defeated but chooses the time and the appropriate action. He remains in control of himself and his situation. This is not a defeat or a setback but a tactical decision and he decides when to re-enter the battle. So here we have contrary advice: PPO ('Persistence Pays Off') and a decision to withdraw and rest. Your subconscious, a dream or a flash of inspiration will tell you which is right – logic is not helpful here because in such decisions we are dealing with our emotions.

 **brilliant** recap

- Motivation is based on three needs – power, affiliation and achievement.

- Identify your strongest need and use this knowledge to help you work on yourself and with others.

- When you lose motivation, because you are human and slippage goes with the territory of personal development, remember to rest, reflect and then to revive.

- Your log book should act as a reminder of all your achievements and how far you have come. It should be one of your best motivational aids.

CHAPTER 12

Gaining support

*S*elf-development and working on being successful on your own is like being a marathon runner: it takes a lot of time, energy and effort. Of course there is a lot of satisfaction in being like Frank Sinatra who 'did it my way'[1], but most people prefer to get 'a little help from their friends'.[2]

And that help can be invaluable because not only do you have the back-up to keep you motivated and on the right track, but often you can find people who have been there before you. Whatever you want, wherever you are going and whatever goals you have, they have experienced the same path and you should seek their wisdom to assist you on your way.

Your network

Support can come from many areas – friends, training programmes, a coach, a mentor – each offering their own brand of help. They will also know people that can help you or point you in the right direction. A good network of support will:

- provide you with objective advice
- give you support and encouragement

---

1 But would he have done it without the backing of the Count Basie Orchestra?
2 As the Beatles did.

- help to keep things in perspective
- help you to enjoy your successes.

And support can come from the most unexpected places. From now on regard every new person you meet as someone who might be able to help you in the future by becoming part of your network and you theirs. It's important to make it a reciprocal relationship so that you both feel supported towards achieving your ambitions.

If you are feeling shy or awkward about asking for help then ask yourself, 'If the positions were reversed, would I be happy to do it for them if I was asked?' And remember, unless you ask you will never get (unless of course it's contagious!).

Who to ask

When thinking about who to approach for support, go for experience every time, especially if you know someone who has been successful in what you want to achieve. Someone who has been there before and can help you avoid the pitfalls and mistakes along the way is invaluable.

brilliant tip

As far as I know there are no universities issuing degrees in personal development but there are lots of people who have achieved or arrived at where you want to go and have 'scar tissue' by making mistakes along their personal journey. So remember, as you make your journey: 'Best advice comes from scar tissue rather than university issue.'

People with experience are invaluable to have in your network.

 **activity**

Developing a support network

Very early in life we quickly learn that 'it's not what you know but who you know' that counts. Achieving success in life is not that easy when you only have yourself to talk to, because you only know what you know and it's difficult to argue with yourself. Here are 25 suggestions for people who would be useful to have in your support network:

1   Someone who is well networked and knows lots of people

2   Someone you can relate to

3   Someone who knows your area of work

4   Someone who is where you want to be

5   Someone who is willing to help

6   Someone who is very positive

7   Someone who is frank

8   Someone who has the skills that you wish to develop

9   Someone who is honest in their criticism

10 Someone in the same profession as you

11 Someone who is good at resourcing

12 Someone that has a lifestyle that you admire

13 Someone who will challenge you

14 Someone who can motivate you

15 Someone who is qualified to give you advice in the areas you need

16 Someone who can help you through bad news/times

17 Someone you trust

18 Someone who is good at giving pragmatic advice

19 Someone who can advise you on relational matters

20 Someone with whom you can have fun

21 Someone who is worldly wise

22 Someone who is creative and good at suggesting options

23 Someone who is realistic

24 Someone you respect

25 Someone who can offer a moral or spiritual perspective.

Think about the five people you admire who between them cover all these attributes and whom you could approach as supporters.

Mentoring

Ulysses, in the Trojan War myth, turned to his great friend Mentor, to whom he entrusted the education of his son Telemachus. This proved to be an invaluable role as Ulysses was kept away from home by mischievous and vexatious gods for a decade. During this time Mentor coached and advised Telemachus in the art of kingship and fulfilled his role so admirably that his name as a development expert has survived for 3000 years.

Many people have experienced the huge advantages of having a mentor, both as a role model and a sage resource for advice on topics such as:

- career moves
- developing self-esteem
- self-promotion
- interpersonal relationships
- work projects and challenges
- forestalling possible errors
- sources of and access to information
- network contacts
- the 'politics' of life and work
- how to present oneself.

For mentoring to be effective, a special relationship of mutual respect between protégé and mentor needs to be in place so that both parties can benefit from the relationship.

Selecting a mentor

Many companies have set up formal mentoring programmes, but if your employer does not enjoy the advantages of such a system there is no reason why you should not find your own. Most successful adults are willing to share the 'secrets of their success' and find it flattering to be asked to do so.

The things to look for in a mentor include someone who:

- has been successful in your chosen field of endeavour
- enjoys a good professional reputation
- can clarify your goals and aspirations
- you can respect
- is empathetic
- is a good listener
- can motivate you
- you can form a close relationship with
- is perceptive and understanding
- can give honest and constructive feedback
- has a good network in your field
- will give you their time on a regular basis
- will respond to your needs
- you can trust
- will develop and challenge you rather than just teach
- can advise on your goals and ambitions
- can act confidentially
- is ideally about 15 years older than you.

If your mentor has most of the above attributes then they could probably walk on water and calm any storm. The most important thing is to find someone with whom you have synergy and mutual respect.

Things to avoid in a mentor include someone who:

● has just taken up a new position (they will not have time to see you despite what they might tell you)

● is so high up in your field, function or sector that you find it difficult to relate to one another

● is not popular – it's a warning that they have difficulty motivating their staff and/or peers

● has unreasonable expectations of themselves and others

● is boastful, arrogant and/or talks too much, losing sight of you as the focus.

Mentoring sessions

Ideally, to begin with, it's most helpful to meet weekly for the first month if schedules and commitments allow. These intensive initial meetings will give both parties the opportunity to really get to know each other and for the protégé be able to outline their situation, their needs and their expectations. During this period, mutual expectations are agreed, together with a form of contract (detailing what can or can't be discussed, how the process might be terminated, mutual confidentiality, etc.) for each party and a timetable for possible meetings.

Occasionally, during this initial phase, should the relationship not live up to the original expectations of either party it can be ended without much embarrassment, pain or danger to either side. As we have said, synergy between mentor and protégé is crucial if mentoring is going to be successful for you both.

Once the start-up stage has been completed, after say one or two months, then periods between meetings can be extended to a month. (Although some people meet once a quarter, I would not recommend fewer meetings than this.)

As you are the protégé, it will be useful to record the action and learning points of your sessions with your mentor and also record your progress. This will form the initial agenda to be discussed at your next meeting. So I'm afraid you'll need another log book.

Mentoring agenda

It is usually the protégé's job to set the agenda and it's helpful for the mentor if they can have the agenda a few days before the meeting so that they have time to prepare. The most popular topics include:

- taking stock of skills and competences
- personal relationships, both social and work
- understanding life and business issues
- errors of judgement
- challenges currently being faced
- reflection on past successes and failures to ensure learning
- consideration of networking opportunities
- developing short-, medium- and long-term goals
- personal promotion and self-presentation
- construction of future strategies
- appropriate qualifications, courses and programmes
- advice on what experience to gain for maximum development and opportunities
- sources and access to information and contacts
- career opportunities.

In all of this it's the protégé's responsibility to take control of their own development. It's not the job of the mentor to teach but to guide and encourage the protégé to work things out for themselves and discuss alternatives, thus ensuring total ownership of the mentoring development experience.

How to prepare for a meeting

In preparation for a meeting with your mentor it will be useful for you to ask yourself some or all of the following questions:

- What have I done since we last met?
- What have I done differently?
- What have I found difficult?
- What have I found easy?
- What have I found interesting?
- What skills have I developed?
- How have I grown my network?
- What have I read?
- What have I learnt?
- What do I want to discuss with my mentor?

Terminating the relationship

On a semi-regular basis, say every six months, both parties should take stock of how the relationship and the work is progressing. This enables both parties to reaffirm their expectations and perhaps negotiate new ones. There should be no difficulty or embarrassment if either party feels that the process has come full circle.

Nothing lasts forever and one of the dangers of mentoring is that as a protégé you can become dependent on your mentor.

Fledglings have to learn to fly and sometimes they have to be pushed out of the nest to do so. A good mentor will know and inform their protégé that the time has come for them to fly solo. Usually the friendship that has been established over the months then continues on an informal basis. Most mentors are happy to provide an 'after-sales service' should their protégé need their help on a topic or difficulty. Assistance is usually given out of friendship.

brilliant recap

- Support will keep you motivated and help you avoid potential pitfalls.

- A good support system gives you objective advice, encouragement, perspective and a way to mark success.

- Everyone you meet is a potential supporter.

- Mentoring offers one of the best forms of support.

- Synergy and mutual respect is crucial between you and your mentor.

- It's your development – so you set the agenda and control the course.

PART 2

Getting development fit

Now that we have done the hard yards on rediscovering who we are and what we want, and considered how we might get there, this next stage is about ensuring that we are fit for the journey. As we have said, most people could run a marathon, but most people couldn't run the 26 miles 385 yards tomorrow. However, with six months of determined training first they would be in good shape to try. It is just the same with personal development – we need to get ourselves physically and mentally fit for our personal development marathon.

So in this part we will work on the self-esteem, self-confidence and stress management upon which we will build our new selves. Nothing comes easily so we will also prepare ourselves for life's demolition crew, the team that gets contracted out whenever we attempt any new personal development challenge. The crew has the objective of corrupting our vision and disrupting our plans. Remember those critical voices that run around in our head telling us we should take the easy road and stay the way we are. Now once you know and anticipate these enemies of progress you will be in good shape to convert those inevitable setbacks and failures into future successes.

CHAPTER 13

Achieving
self-esteem

What holds us back?

We have a predicament in that life is not fair. Each of us has inherited the way our genetic die was thrown and how it fell on the green baize of life. Of course, if we were able to select all four grandparents we could almost be guaranteed a die roll of six. But, in a very true sense, at conception we get the genes we have to 'wear' for life. We could probably score another six if we could choose parents who were wonderfully gifted intellectually and emotionally, who enjoyed good health and were gifted in nurturing skills. It would be an added bonus if they enjoyed a comfortable financial status and let us share in it. But as we know, things can and frequently do go wrong and self-esteem is one of the prime candidates to be adversely affected. It is the handbrake on life's opportunities. It is those inner voices all over again:

'I could never …
  'I'm too old/young to …'
    'I'm not qualified to …'
      'I don't deserve …'
        'I'm not clever enough …'
          'I'm not good enough …'

The negative voices go on and on, and our development does not go on at all.

Whichever way our genetic 'life die' falls we all get the same unit of self-esteem. Tall or short, thin or fat, clever or dull, strong or weak, we all inherit one unit each of self-esteem and each unit is the same. The problems start happening when we come screaming out of the womb.

As soon as our brains can think beyond food, comfort and loving physical contact, we begin comparing ourselves with others and the assessment game begins. In fact, the way we are different or the same as others helps us develop a self-concept. Once these comparisons start, our self-esteem either waxes or wanes.

Along the way, we also experience unexplained failures and are given inappropriate messages about who we are, through which we struggle to comprehend our identities. For example, two professional caring and loving parents support their only child as very best they can, but he is expelled from three schools, is in trouble with he law at 14, runs away from home at 15, is a drug addict at 16 and is killed in a gang fight a year later. Here the parents' self-esteem and confidence suffers a huge blow. They are haunted by the question: 'Where did we go wrong?' Perceived emotions trump facts every time, ensuring the esteem of these parents is severely damaged with piercing inner voices continually repeating such things as 'I must be an inadequate parent', 'I'm not fit to bring children into the world', 'I must be hopeless'.

'If you compare yourself with others, you may become vain and bitter; for always there will be greater and lesser persons than yourself.'

Max Ehrmann, American writer

Culture and self-esteem

And there is something else that has an excessive effect on our single unit of self-esteem – our culture. Culture is like the bodywork of a car that surrounds the engine. Culture decides what is acceptable and what is not; what is success and what is not; what is beautiful and what is not; what is of value and what is not. It's not always right or fair but culture, be it national, local or even at school through bullying, is a strong force adversely affecting our self-esteem. Nobody would blink an eye if Rosa Parks sat wherever she wanted on a bus today, but in 1955 this small act sparked a revolution. In 1895 the British establishment crushed the genius that was Oscar Wilde because of his sexuality, while today we'd be celebrating his civil partnership. A fabulous example of a cultural transition was demonstrated by the publication in 1961 of John Howard Griffin's seminal book *Black Like Me* which devastated thinking white America and was the progenitor of the much needed equality that was to come.

 'No one can get you to feel inferior without your consent.'

Eleanor Roosevelt

Building your self-esteem

Strategy 1: no comparisons – you are who you are

Life is not about living up to the expectation of others, no matter how precious they are to you. Nor is it about how much you have amassed, whatever society values, such as the trappings of success, be they money, property or the world's accolades. Nor are you your job title.

Ask people who they are and 99 times out of 100 they will respond with a job title that some organisation or profession has given them. Self-esteem is not dependent on your job. I'd go so far as to say it's dangerous to allow yourself to become identified by what you do. What happens if you lose your job through no fault of your own? What if you are made redundant or the company goes bust? What are you then? There is little self-esteem behind the statement 'I used to be a ...'

'I would rather be an original copy of myself than a second-hand copy of someone else.'

Eleanor Roosevelt

Strategy 2: acceptance

You have been given a body, you have developed a personality, acquired some skills and competences and that is it. Whether you like your body or not, or wish you were taller, shorter, thinner, fatter, leaner, muscular, blonde or brunette is not relevant. You have what you have, so accept it. For the most part it's not constructive for self-development to spend your life wishing for things you cannot change, nor is it emotionally helpful.

Occasional daydreaming about being a superstar, however you conceive that notion, can be both inspiring and motivating, even psychologically healthy. But you must tread carefully between the line of healthy ambition and allowing your unrealistic fantasies to become toxic, especially as you realise you are probably not one of the few people that society rates as prestigious, intellectual, courageous, handsome or beautiful. This can only lead to your self-esteem being corroded and again you will become a lesser person for it. But enough of this negativity!

'All men dream: but not equally.
Those who dream by night in the dusty
recesses of their minds
wake in the day to find that it was vanity;
But the dreamers of the day are dangerous men,
for they may act their dream with open eyes,
to make it possible.'

T.E. Lawrence, army officer (Lawrence of Arabia),
Seven Pillars of Wisdom

Strategy 3: go easy on yourself

There are enough people in the world who will gladly remind us of our errors and mistakes. There's no need for you to become a card-carrying member of life's 'beat up union'. After all, the only people who can return no recent mistakes on life's scorecard all have permanent abodes in boxes six feet under. Mistakes, errors and poor judgements are proof that we are alive, well and doing the best we can with what we have at the time.

No one deliberately makes a fool out of themselves or sets out to make errors or misjudgements. These are life lessons and usually life keeps presenting them to us again and again until we learn from them. Such lessons are nothing to do with self-esteem.

 'Beyond a wholesome discipline, be gentle with yourself.'

'Desiderata' by Max Ehrmann

If you are wrong or in error, say sorry, apologise and move on. And if you find that the other person is still not happy, ask them what else you can do to make amends. In all likelihood there is nothing, they just need extra reassurance of your sincerity.

Life's formula would appear to be:

Act, error, learn;

Act, error, learn;

Act, error, learn;

with the development strategy being not to make the same error again.

Strategy 4: judge not

This is the opposite side of the coin from making unfavourable comparisons of yourself against others. When you make judgements about others, you are into the comparison game again, letting your ego run in the wrong direction with the comparison/ judgement: 'I am better than him/her because ...'. Well, no, not really, because whoever threw your life die did a better job for you than your comparison person or group in terms of intelligence, health, background or opportunity.

 'Humility does not mean thinking less of yourself than of other people, nor does it mean having a low opinion of your own gifts. It means freedom from thinking about yourself at all.'

William Temple, Archbishop of Canterbury 1942–44

'There are two kinds of egotists: those who admit it, and the rest of us.'

Laurence J. Peter, educator

It's not easy because who we are is very much influenced by who we are not. We see ourselves as someone other. At a simple level: 'I am a male because I am not female.' However, the same logic follows with 'I'm not someone who is on welfare, lives in a slum or wears clothes from charity shops and consequently I must be better, more important, and more significant ...' Again, no, not really. Nor does it work if you came from a welfare home in a slum area and became a huge entrepreneurial success. That is most laudable and may give you a boost to your unit of self-esteem, especially since the world values wealth, but it does not make you a better person.

'Do not judge yourself or others when attempting to preserve your self-esteem.'

Anon

'If you really think you are somebody then put your head in a bucket of water, withdraw it, look back in the bucket and contemplate the size of the hole that your head has made.'

My Welsh father-in-law (who can't remember where he heard it)

Strategy 5: deal with negative criticism

Criticism can be useful, especially when it's constructive. However, when its intent is to put you down, your self-esteem will be in for some dents. Some people need to put others down in a poor attempt to make themselves superior. Usually, if they need to do this it's for their own ego needs and they get very good at it with all the practice they give themselves at the expense of others. Remember, they are still playing the comparison game and will be suffering from a good dose of low self-esteem themselves.

In life, the unhealthy criticism you can expect will include:

1 inappropriate and/or cruel insults

2 unwanted physical contact

3 verbal and non-verbal attempts to intimidate

4 status and achievement put-downs

5 political sabotage

6 ridicule in both private and public situations

7 being the butt of jokes

8 being at the unwanted end of sarcasm

9 aggressive interruptions and put-downs

10 interference with your personal property

11 aspersions about your gender, ethnicity, colour, background, experience, etc.

12 challenges on your competence

13 barring you from the 'in group'.

A real dirty baker's dozen, but I'm sure that there is a whole bakery out there of similar comments just waiting to be given to you for free.

Some relief is at hand. People who engage in such unacceptable behaviour are very much creatures of habit. Just as when you hear thunder you get your umbrella and raincoat, when those people begin to rain down their 'put downs' you can be prepared. Like a punch in the stomach, if you can flex your abs it doesn't hurt as much.

> Remember the children's nursery rhyme which comes in two versions:
>
> Sticks and stones
> Will break my bones
> But names will never hurt me.
>
> *or*
>
> Sticks and stones
> May break my bones
> But words will never hurt me
>
> **A fantastic comeback!**

For totally inappropriate, rude or just plain silly criticism, one of the most powerful, shortest and by far the easiest response is not to ignore it – your silence might be interpreted as acceptance, which will only massage the critic's ego and encourage repeat behaviour – but to make the simple comment: **'That was**

an interesting statement/comment and I wonder why you found it necessary to make it?' 'Wonder' and 'why' are two very authoritative words and when this question is aimed unexpectedly, it is very difficult for the critic to answer without either making their justification incriminating or making themselves look very silly.

Strategy 6: be rational not emotional

Sometimes it's important to evaluate the criticism rationally to discover whether this is something you should take to heart and act upon, or just a barb sent your way by someone who should be looking at their own inadequacies. So before you give criticism of your behaviour the power to damage your self-esteem, here are some questions you might reflect upon:

- How qualified is the person to make such a statement?
- Are you aware that you behave in this way (maybe this is constructive criticism)?
- Is this behaviour frequent or significant enough for you to give it your attention?
- If you changed this behaviour are there any advantages that would accrue to you or is it in your interest to continue to be the way you are?
- If you wanted, is this behaviour something you could change?
- Changing behaviour is not easy, so are you prepared to put in the effort and psychological cost that is required to change?

Only bother reflecting on criticism that is about your specific behaviour – in other words, behaviour that can be observed. Non-specific feedback using 'fat words' is not worth thinking about. For instance, take the statement 'You are too quiet'. This has the 'fat' word 'quiet' and consequently really does not mean very much. What does 'quiet' mean in specific behavioural terms?

- That they cannot hear you?
- That you speak too softly?
- That you speak in a monotone?
- That the frequency of your speech is too ponderous?
- That you are hesitant when you speak?
- That you should express your opinions more often?
- That you do not express your emotions?
- That you do not show appreciation at some entertainment event that you have enjoyed?

If you think you might benefit from what lies beneath the fat words, and you would like to explore the 'fat comment', then you can ask, 'Please help me here – in what way specifically am I too quiet?' Then, if you get the specifics and the facts that support the criticism, you can do something useful about it, if you feel it's the right thing to do.

As a final point here, always challenge absolute comments: 'You always …', 'Every time you …', 'All you do is …', 'You constantly …' Here you just throw back the words as a question: 'Every?' 'Always?', and so on. The advantage here is that whilst your behaviour might justify the comment, no one is that consistent. It may be a significant aspect of your behaviour which needs attention or it could be very infrequent. Asking for examples encourages the other person to give you specific instances so that you can assess to what extent (if at all) you need to act on their criticism. If no examples are forthcoming then their criticism falls away, counting for nothing.

Strategy 7: deal with positive criticism

Some people with low self-esteem have difficulty with posi-tive criticism or compliments because they wear permanent anti-esteem earplugs. Compliments are vacuumed up, like cat hair on a Persian carpet, rather than accepted.

It's important here to note the difference between pride and self-esteem. Self-esteem is the ability to recognise your talents. Pride, on the other hand, is the need to demonstrate how wonderful you are, continually assuming that you are better than everyone else.

Sabotaging praise with 'anyone could do it' just corrodes your self-esteem and you are also being dismissive of the friend or colleague who recognised your talent or achievement and wants to congratulate you. Such behaviour is unlikely to encourage the person to be so appreciative in the future.

Praise and compliments are the lifeblood needed to confirm, maintain and grow your self-esteem; failing to acknowledge them will haemorrhage the little which you still have.

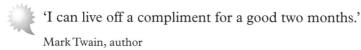 'I can live off a compliment for a good two months.'

Mark Twain, author

'Low self-esteem is like driving through life with your hand-break on.'

Maxwell Maltz, author of *Psycho-Cybernetics*

'Never bend your head. Always hold it high. Look the world straight in the face.'

Helen Keller

'Nothing builds self-esteem and self-confidence like accomplishment.'

Thomas Carlyle, Scottish satirical writer

'I used to be arrogant but now I know I'm perfect.'

Max Eggert

Self-esteem is one of the cornerstones to personal development. Work on it and build a strong sense of your place in the world and you will find it much easier to achieve your goals. Not only that, but you will be able to take risks and recover from failure, criticism or embarrassment because you will have the necessary psychological strength.

brilliant recap

- Everyone has self-esteem at birth. Your self-esteem is not dependent on the opinion of others.
- You are a person not your job title, or how much you have or earn, or how society regards you.
- It's not healthy to compare yourself with others.
- Accept what nature has given you.
- Do not judge yourself too harshly.
- Do not judge others.
- Evaluate negative criticism.
- Be rational and not emotional.
- Challenge absolute criticisms.
- Accept and enjoy compliments.

CHAPTER 14

Achieving self-confidence

'Doctor, I am so sorry to trouble you. I have this real inferiority complex ... but ... it's not a very big one!'

Once you have mastered and nurtured your self-esteem, the next stage in your self-development programme is to spend some time with the first cousin of self-esteem: self-confidence.

Self-confidence comes under several guises including, but not limited to, self-belief, self-assurance and self-regard. Perhaps another way of thinking about it is that self-esteem is internal. It's how you think and feel about yourself. If your self-esteem is strong then this affects how you behave in the world, i.e. your external behaviour. High self-esteem is the engine that drives self-confidence.

With all these shades of meaning it might be helpful to suggest a definition which will clarify the concept:

 **brilliant** definition

Self-confidence

This is the ability to behave with poise and control in both personal and social situations, knowing that this is possible irrespective of your standing in society, your education, ethnicity, sexual orientation or religious and political affiliations.

So self-confidence is essentially an attitude towards self and life in general. It is a conviction about your own abilities – that you have reasonable control over yourself and your life. Since confident individuals have realistic expectations of themselves, which includes recognising and accepting their weaknesses, they do not assume that they are good at everything – they are always ready to learn.

Self-confidence is critical to our psychological wellbeing. Being without confidence is like being the pilot of a plane and realising that you have just run out of fuel – the only way is down. It's healthy to exercise choice and personal preferences in life but it becomes dangerous if we choose not to like ourselves and prefer not to be 'us'. It is of no consequence psychologically to prefer coffee to tea or Beethoven to Bach, but it's not healthy to prefer to be someone other than who you are.

To always judge and criticise yourself is emotionally damaging and leads you to spiral down and, in some extreme cases, into that black hole we call depression.

Are we born with too much or too little of this precious characteristic? Yes and no, but it doesn't matter if we were not given the right genes at birth because it's possible to develop self-confidence since it is not a dispositional trait, but a characteristic. Some psychologists have suggested that self-confidence is something that we act on rather than intrinsically have. Perhaps we should remember that babies, before they can even talk, are certainly not backward in coming forward with great confidence for the things they want. Whatever the cognitive hoops babies struggle to jump through as they work hard to understand their confusing world, I'm sure that thoughts such as:

- 'Because I cry a lot I don't deserve to be fed';
- 'I'm so unattractive no one will cuddle me'; or
- 'I've just soiled myself again – my mother will think I am disgusting and selfish',

will not figure significantly in their cognitive pre-verbal ruminations.

What happened to us? Well, for a whole variety of reasons, we developed voices in our heads. Some of the voices we developed when comparing ourselves to others – 'I'm not as clever/not as good looking/not as fluent', and, later in life, 'not as rich/not as important/not as influential' – and then turning these observations into negative thoughts about ourselves which we believe, and then we behave as if they were true and immutable facts in all future situations.

Getting started

We don't go to the dentist to hear how the enamel and dentine has been eroded and the inner living pulp of the affected tooth is being irritated by bacterial toxins, thus delivering an up-close and very personal toothache – we just want it fixed and our pain to go away. Consequently the 'how' we arrived at our current level of self-confidence is not as important as the 'what' we can do about it.

You might view yourself as a victim of your past (genetics, parents, upbringing or unfortunate significant emotional events). Here we have to think and act as a person who has decided to work on and develop themselves in certain areas of their choosing. You have no choice, you have to go with what you've got and who you are. The best advice is to be like Popeye whose mantra was:

'I yam what I yam and I do what I can because I yam Popeye the Sailor Man.'

By working through this chapter you might begin to think that your particular situation is worse than you first imagined – let me assure you it isn't. So now let's turn to examine self-confidence with particular emphasis on what has the potential to reduce and damage it.

The critical voices from childhood

Regrettably, sometimes, the voices were 'planted' in our heads by significant others when we were very young. Parents tell their children they 'are lazy', they 'are disorganised' or, even worse, they 'will not amount to much' or they 'are stupid'. Close family members such as older siblings or grandparents, even friends of the family, through their negative comments can also be guilty. Planting negative thoughts will breed negative voices. By the time you reach adulthood the voices are firmly anchored into your subconscious; you believe they are true and act accordingly.

Way back in 600 BC the Book of Proverbs states:

'As a man thinks in his heart, so is he.'

(23:7)

Personally, as I'm dyslexic, I was instructed, at the age of eight, by my teacher, to stand in front of the class and say three times in a loud voice, 'I am stupid, stupid, stupid.' Although I managed it through my tears, in a way it was great because being stupid encouraged me to put all my efforts into sport. It was a great relief to hear my father say on production of my school report gleaming with academic failures, 'Never mind, son, it takes a good brain to resist education.' However, this 'you are stupid' voice was very persistent, bubbling up at regular intervals. Thinking of myself as stupid was still ringing in my ears during my late teens and early twenties. It was not until I was 45 with three degrees, several postgrad diplomas and, at that time, 44 letters after my name parading my credentials, that I realised that I was stupid in collecting qualifications and even more stupid to have had that voice embedded in my brain for 37 years. It was a huge relief to say, 'Stuff night school, I want to play the guitar; stuff all this academic study, I want to ride horses.'

Typical voices

Inappropriate critical voices that are dumped upon us, sometimes with extremely adverse effects on our self-confidence, might include:

- I am ugly.
- I am scatterbrained.
- I am untidy.
- I am lazy.
- I am good for nothing.
- I am stupid.
- I am selfish.

- I am weak.
- I am cowardly.
- I am boring.
- I am moody.
- I am unreliable.
- I am thick or stupid.
- I am socially inept.

Yours not here ? Then please add it to the list to recognise the enemy.

These are just some of the inappropriate 'I am' voices and statements that abound in our heads and affect our lives and development adversely.

Many children of the last century were brought up with the nursery rhyme:

'What are little boys made of?
Slugs and snails, and puppy-dogs' tails,
That's what little boys are made of.
What are little girls made of?
Sugar and spice, and everything nice,
That's what little girls are made of.'

Robert Southey (who became Poet Laureate in England in 1813)

So it's not surprising that some people are victims of 'cultural voices' such as:

- 'Girls are not supposed to be clever.'
- 'Girls are not good at maths.'

- 'Men are not supposed to show their emotions.'
- 'Men don't cry.'

All of us have voices in our heads. Ask anyone the question, 'Do you have voices in your head?' and unless they say 'Yes' immediately, you can then say to them, 'I bet you are saying to yourself, "Do I have voices in my head?"'. They will laugh because we all have those voices.

And here we can see, hear and feel the danger of our self-confidence just dribbling away if we allow such negative statements to rattle around in our subconscious, imbue us with self-doubt and attempt to scuttle our self-belief.

We will look at how to banish these confidence terrorists but, for me, Henry Ford stated it perfectly with:

'If you think you are or if you think you are not; you are right.'

What he actually said was 'If you think you can or think you can't, you're right', but I don't think he would mind the adaption!

The negative voices we develop for ourselves

Sometimes we are our own worst enemy. To the detriment of our self-confidence we frequently donate and bequeath these pernicious voices to ourselves through our own faulty thinking. The sequence of events leading up to the birth of these troubling inner demons is usually that we have tried to do something different or experiment with a new behaviour only to find ourselves in a situation where it all goes pear-shaped. As we venture to rationalise or understand this unwanted fruit of failure we become victims of our own faulty thinking. It comes in at least six different and inappropriate thought disguises.

Here are some examples of what we can do to ourselves:

Once to always

If we fail once then we will always fail. Thus we generalise from one instance to all similar future situations.

'I made a poor speech two years ago. I'm definitely not good at public speaking.'

Blue glasses

Rejecting all praise and recalling only the bad things. When your glasses are tinted blue then the bottles of life are, at best, half empty!

'That was a great speech!'

'Yes, but I don't think I got my message across.'

It's all about me

Making everything your responsibility; whatever goes wrong then it must be your fault.

'I know lots of people were late. I should have known that the snow was so bad. I should have started my speech much later; it's entirely my fault.'

The fortune teller

This is where you have fully developed your nascent gift of being able to read other people's minds.

'I just know, by looking at them, that they thought my speech was nonsense.'

Self-flagellation

You always feel the need to apologise for everything that ever goes wrong.

'I'm so sorry that your equipment failed during my speech. It's my

fault: I should have asked you to double-check it before I went on. I'm so sorry.'

Either ... or

Here you polarise your reasoning about your performance or behaviour so that you were either absolutely fantastic or a total failure. For you there is no middle ground of success. You either give your self an 'A plus' or an 'F minus', because your actions are judged by yourself to be either black or white. There are no shades of grey in your self-evaluation pallet.

'I stumbled over the pronunciation of Alkylphenol Polyethoxylate when talking in front of my peers, so I must be totally useless at giving presentations!'

When you employ this faulty thinking about yourself the internal critic claims yet another victory, your confidence oozes down into your black hole of self-doubt and you excuse yourself from facing similar situations where you 'failed'. Low self-confidence goes hand in hand with self-restriction.

Here are a dirty dozen ways we limit ourselves, but I'm sure there are some more from those negative voices in your own head as well as mine:

1 I will never be popular.

2 I will never be any good.

3 I will never get married.

4 I will never amount to much.

5 I will never be a success.

6 I will never get another job.

7 I will never pass an exam.

8 I will never be happy.

9 I will never be able to dance or act or sing.

10 I will never be good at sport or social things.

11 I will never be able to please my partner.

12 I will never achieve the respect of my peers.

 **brilliant** activity

How self-confident are you?

Here is a very quick little questionnaire. There are no right or wrong answers, but remember if your answers are not the truth you will not get a true score, so be honest with yourself!

1 Do you feel that most people are better than you at most things?

Usually ☐   Sometimes ☐   Never ☐

2 Do you drink, eat or smoke more than you should?

Usually ☐   Sometimes ☐   Never ☐

3 Do you take all criticism to heart?

Usually ☐   Sometimes ☐   Never ☐

4 Do you have doubts about the way you look?

Usually ☐   Sometimes ☐   Never ☐

5 Do you frequently feel socially inept?

Usually ☐   Sometimes ☐   Never ☐

6 Do you hold yourself back from trying new things?

Usually ☐   Sometimes ☐   Never ☐

7 Do you worry about making new relationships?

Usually ☐   Sometimes ☐   Never ☐

8 Do you think that people talk or laugh about you?

Usually ☐   Sometimes ☐   Never ☐

▶

9 Do you get concerned about whether people like you or not?

Usually ☐   Sometimes ☐   Never ☐

10 Do you apologise a lot?

Usually ☐   Sometimes ☐   Never ☐

11 Do you worry about upsetting people?

Usually ☐   Sometimes ☐   Never ☐

12 Do you frequently doubt your ability?

Usually ☐   Sometimes ☐   Never ☐

Scoring:

Give yourself 1 for never, 2 for sometimes and 3 for usually.

Now add up your scores:

30–36: You are quite low on self-confidence and self-promotion activities are likely to be difficult for you.

24–29: On occasions you lack self-confidence.

20–23: You are about the same as most people in the self-confidence stakes.

17–20: You are a self-confident person.

12–16: You may be suffering from motivated distortion (psych jargon for fibbing on the questionnaire!) or, worse, possibly hubris – do the questionnaire again – no one is that confident!

If you genuinely scored less than 17 you might like to skip this section of the book rather than spending valuable time on what you cannot do!

The tyranny of 'must's', 'ought's' and 'should's'

One more trick of the internal voice critic is the tyranny of 'must's', 'ought's' and 'should's' that we get given by our family upbringing, education and culture. How many of these are familiar?

- I must work hard.
- I must respect my elders.
- I must be good.
- I must be perfect.
- I ought to be nice to everyone.
- I ought to act like a man (or a woman).
- I must be reasonable.
- I ought not to complain.
- I should always tell the truth.
- I should be a perfect parent.
- I should always be giving.

There are also some 'don'ts' which are just as tyrannical:

- Don't interrupt.
- Don't talk back.
- Don't leave things unfinished.
- Don't be angry.
- Don't ask silly questions.
- Don't rock the boat.
- Don't get upset.

Not that all such imperatives are inappropriate, especially those that come mainly from our culture and experience. So you would be wise, for example:

- not to put yourself or others in danger of harm
- to drive on the left-hand side of the road in Britain, Malta, Hong Kong and Australia
- to only gamble with what you can afford to lose
- to not drink and drive
- to only ever negotiate from power
- to trust everyone but always lock your car
- to remember that if you screw someone they will screw you – eventually
- to always be polite to the police and parking attendants
- not to argue with a person with a loaded submachine gun.

Frivolous, but you know what I mean. None of these axioms will endanger your self-confidence, in fact, some of them might be very helpful.

 **tip**

Be careful not to 'should' all over yourself, and it's not helpful to let others 'should' all over you either.

Why do we take notice of the critical voices?

It's surprising that we listen to these inner voices, especially when they do our self-confidence so much harm. But there are two compelling reasons:

We listen because those we loved and/or respected told us to

Our parents, or those emotionally significant to us, drummed it into us that we must, ought to and should show respect and accept what they told us. It was a trade since we needed their love, approval and recognition. Emotionally it's very difficult to come to the conclusion that your parents have feet of clay and in some things they are definitely wrong.

We listen because it's better to be safe than sorry

We don't want to take the untried risk of changing – although inadequate, we feel safe in the thick shells of our inadequacies: 'If it ain't broke why improve it?'

We can excuse our behaviour because the inner voice confirms who we are; it alleviates our responsibility for not trying:

- 'Great, if I'm stupid why should I even attempt to understand anything?'
- 'Hooray, I'm off the hook again, where is my Xbox?'

The outcomes are predictable. If you believe that, 'Because I'm socially inept they will not invite me', when you don't get the invite you are not surprised because you predicted your omission on the social list and this confirms your inner voice.

Not only is this difficult but the prize for persistence goes to this inner critic in that it never leaves us alone and we, for the most part, can't but stop and listen.

An aside

Sometimes this self-protection from not doing something requested of you takes an interesting and amusing turn. On being requested to assist in the post-dinner washing-up, my daughter, who is also challenged in the spelling and writing department, came up with this:

Marisian: 'But, Dad, I don't do washing up.'
Me: 'Why is that, Marisian?'
Marisian: 'Oh, Dad, you know why! It's because I'm dyslexic'.

Now, just as much as this is amusing, it's not much different from an internal voice:

Statement: 'I will never get married.'
Inner question: 'Why won't you ever get married?'
Answer: 'Because I'm shy.'

And this would be amusing if it wasn't true. One claimed incompetence leads to a totally false assumption which has no rational connection, with usually unfortunate outcomes. Remember the Henry Ford quote:

'If you think you can or you think you can't. You are right.'

When does the negative voice strike?

It strikes in certain situations when we are faced with something we have not attempted, for example:

● meeting someone for the first time: 'They won't like me.'

- coming into contact with someone who knows about a recent failure: 'They know how useless I am.'
- wanting to respond when someone has criticised you: 'Be quiet, they're right, I always screw up, better to say nothing.'
- wanting to take a relationship to the next stage (e.g. to invite a person to an event or a date: 'They will never go out with me.')
- having to negotiate with someone: 'I know that they are going to take me to the cleaners.'
- being invited to make a speech: 'This is where I screw up big time.'

In a social situation, if you tell yourself that you will be excluded, guess what? You will be. If you think you are a bad presenter, guess what? You will be. If you think that no one will go on a date with you, guess what? You're going to miss out on a lot of dates.

People whose inner critic tells them that they are unattractive sometimes do nothing to improve their attractiveness and gradually, by letting themselves go and not caring about themselves, they really do become unattractive. In life we are very much our own prophets fulfilling our own expectations.

'Our doubts are traitors and make us lose the good we oft might win, by fearing to attempt.'

William Shakespeare, *Measure for Measure*

Purging the negative voice

Well, that is all the bad news so, before we imitate the hermit crab and scurry back into our protective shell and hide from the world, let's see what is possible to change.

The voices from childhood

It would be wonderful if we could develop a selective deafness to deal with these voices, but unfortunately they have been chiming in our heads for so long that they have become almost hardwired. 'I am disorganised' comes into your head so quickly before you even commence a complicated task. Then you say to yourself, 'I must not be disorganised about this.' But here is the thing; the brain has difficulties when dealing with negatives because it has to unpack them first. If you tell yourself, 'I must not be disorganised', your brain has to think about being 'disorganised' first before it can reverse it and think of the positive 'organised' state. Rather like a parent telling a child, 'Don't play in the road', the embedded sentence which the child hears first is, 'Play in the road.' How much better to say, 'Play in the park.' So what to do?

Strategy 1: naming the critics

I had a friend once who was able to get all her voices out of her head and onto her shoulder as if they were parrots. On reflection she could recognise many of them. There was her mother: 'You are lazy', 'You will never be a success.' There was her jealous elder sister: 'You are ugly.' There was her teacher: 'You will never come to anything.' There was her first boyfriend: 'You will never be any good at relationships.' So many parrots, but who the voice belonged to was recognised.

Now my friend could say to herself when the parrot spoke, 'I hear you, Mother, but you are wrong', or she could just choose to knock the parrot (aka the person) off its perch on her shoulder, or she could choose to listen.

I have worked with captains of industry, top civil servants and even generals and, guess what, as successful as they are, they all had negative inner voices concerning their abilities. Here is an actual quote from a brigadier with whom I worked whose inner voice was 'I am not good at strategy.'

You will remember that the conversation went like this: 'If I was as good at strategy as Sir Peter over there, I would have made general.' Where did that come from? Perhaps, when the brigadier was just a junior subaltern, his then captain, who he admired greatly, had told him during a review that his strategic ability was poor.

So we have the nine-stage process shown in the diagram.

1. Significant person

2. Negative statement

3. Statement internalised

4. Negative performance since the statement is believed

5. Personal failure because of negative performance

6. Confirmation of internal negative concept

7. External confirmation of negative statement

8. Self-justification

9. Negative statement is reinforced

One wonders how much further up the hierarchy the brigadier would have risen if he had said to himself when he had the opportunity to be strategic, 'I hear you, Captain, but I choose to ignore you because I have worked on my abilities, taken advice from my mentors and read extensively.'

 **brilliant** tip

List all the negative voices that you have and then work hard on discovering who the significant person behind them is. Your negative voices can come from all sorts of people including, but not limited to:

your parents	boyfriend
your step-parents	girlfriend
your foster parents	lover
older or younger siblings	an adult important to your parents
aunt	
uncle	a role model
grandparents	someone you admire(d) greatly
nanny	
childminder	youth club leader
infant teacher	sport coach
priest or pastor	your manager
a friend	doctor.

Once you recognise the owner of the voice it's much easier to deal with and eradicate it.

If you cannot recognise where the voice is coming from, no matter, just give it a name and use it when necessary: 'Oh here comes "Big Mouth" trying to put me down again.'

Strategy 2: the past does not equal the past

Just because you have failed before does not necessarily mean that you will fail again. In life you quickly learn what you can and can't do. But one failure doesn't mean continual failure. It gives you experience of how to tackle the opportunity again in terms of learning preparation and practice (see below).

Just as when we grow physically we can reach further, so as we journey through life with all its lessons we are better equipped to try again. If you concentrate and worry about what happened in the past then you become closed and shut to new opportunities that life presents. It's always easier to say 'No' to opportunity, but you miss a lot and dive into the pit of self-justification.

Strategy 3: doing reversals

Has there ever been a time when a disappointment has turned out to be a blessing? Think of the boyfriend or girlfriend who dumped you, or the job you didn't get – have you now moved onto bigger and better things because of those setbacks?

On many occasions, in retrospect a difficulty has turned out to be a blessing in disguise. A reversal is discovering the silver lining of the dark cloud. It's a way of putting a stop sign in front of your inner critic and instead getting your mind to look at the benefits you will have gained. Should you be criticised or should something happen to you which initially disappoints you, makes you feel inadequate or knocks your self-confidence, then this reversal strategy works very well.

 **example**

Here are some examples of reversals:

- 'I was not invited to the party.'
- → 'Good, it means I can spend time with my special friend, which will be much better.'

- 'I don't know much about literature.'
- → 'That is true, but I prefer to spend my time listening to music, about which I'm exceptionally knowledgeable.'

- 'Jenny doesn't like me.'
- → 'That's unfortunate, but I can't expect everyone to like me. I have lots of personal friends so Jenny is not that important and it is her loss anyway.'

- 'Bridge is too complicated and intellectual for me.'
- → 'It might be, but I play a mean game of chess and five-card stud poker.'
- 'I don't have a boyfriend/girlfriend.'
- → 'That is true currently because I have very high standards and there are still lots more "fish" in the sea.'

Strategy 4: being specific

Here you take apart the content of the critical voice, being very specific about what is true but then balancing it within the total context, which is also true. Remembering what was covered in dealing with 'fat' words, here are some examples:

'I'm socially inept'
Fact: I am anxious about meeting new people for the first time, but once the ice is broken and I have got to know them, then my contribution to the discussion is as good as anyone's, my views are accepted and my company is enjoyed. So, I am socially competent.

'I'm not attractive'
Fact: I am shorter than average and I'm not as fit as I could be but I have lovely skin and hair and many people have complimented me on my dress sense. So, I am attractive.

'I'm scatterbrained'
Fact: I do find it difficult to understand complicated new systems but, once I have mastered the process, I've no difficulty at all. In fact I have trained new staff in many of the systems that I initially found difficult. So I am organised.

'I'm lazy'
Fact: I am lazy but only in doing those things that I am not interested in. In topics or things I find interesting or I think are important, I'm highly motivated.

'I'm moody'

Fact: Yes, sometimes I can be if I'm tired or have too much on my plate, but at all other times I'm on an even keel and people seek my company and invite me to their social gatherings. So, in general I'm calm and even-tempered.

Notice in all the above examples that the conclusion (fact) is always written in the positive. For example, 'I am attractive' is written in preference to 'I am not unattractive', so you avoid thinking about the negative before you can get to the positive implication.

Strategy 5: getting a counter voice

If you are fortunate you can be given, by somebody who is close to you, a positive voice which will wipe out and reverse the negative voice. Here is an example, a self-disclosure about my spelling ability:

Teacher:	'Eggert, you are stupid, stupid, stupid. What are you?'
My father:	'Never mind son, it takes a good brain to resist an education.'
Inner voice:	'Being challenged in my ability to spell does not equate with stupidity and I have been blessed with a good brain.'

Strategy 6: focus on your strengths

Make a list of all the things you are proud of, together with a list of your achievements. (These should already be in your log book from a previous activity.) What are the common threads in your list? What does it say about what you are good at? Give yourself credit for what you have done and, when doubts strike, revisit your list.

Strategy 7: self-evaluation

You are not the sum of other people's views of you. Evaluate yourself and your behaviour independently of others. Do not give credence to the criticism of others but evaluate it and take on board what you find useful.

Strategy 8: preparation

If you lack confidence in doing certain things such as giving a speech, wanting to persuade someone, leading a project, and so on, then you would do well to prepare far more diligently than most other people. Do your research, develop contingency plans, practise talking out loud to yourself and ask yourself lots of 'what if' questions so that you can be really on top of what you are going to do.

Strategy 9: take risks

Of course, doing new things and being successful is a great boost to self-confidence. Should you fail, then rejoice, because life has just given you another learning opportunity. It's not always possible to learn from others. In failing, you give yourself a unique learning opportunity. As we have said before, 'you get things right by getting them wrong.' Just think, when you were a baby, you fell on your bottom hundreds of times but persistence paid off and it was not long before you were walking.

Also, when you fail you realise that it's not the end of the world – the sky did not fall. Not only do people who are important to you still love and like you despite your failure, but when you try again they will admire you.

 'Confidence comes not from always being right but from not fearing to be wrong.'

Peter T. McIntyre, lithographic artist

Strategy 10: make a commitment to yourself

Make an unequivocal promise to yourself that you are totally dedicated to acting confidently. This may sound like 'fake it till you make it' but just as belief turns into behaviour so, in a similar way, behaviour turns into beliefs.

 **tips**

> Slowly begin to stretch yourself in your personal goals. Increase your motivation and keep up your self-talk to succeed and you will be surprised at what you can achieve. Be realistic in what you want to achieve, set your mind to it and, in the words of the Nike slogan: 'Just do it.'
>
> Smile. Self-confident people are self-assured and positive. We smile when we are happy so smile appropriately when with others – nobody grins all the time. Smiling will make you appear confident and people will treat you as such, and this feedback will help you become more confident.

 **activity**

Building self-confidence[1]

This activity is useful in identifying your various capabilities and positive attributes. After you have completed the following statements you might like to share your answers with a friend or someone who knows you well and who could probably suggest some additions. Complete the sentences that follow:

1 Adapted from Robert C. Pozen, *Extreme Productivity: Boost Your Results, Reduce Your Hours*, Harper Business (2012).

Something I do well is _____

_____

Something I'm complimented on is _____

_____

At work I am good at _____

_____

I am proud that at work I _____

_____

My greatest strength at work is _____

_____

At work I can help others to _____

_____

My greatest strength outside work is _____

_____

What I like best about myself is _____

_____

I have the power to _____

_____

I was able to decide to _____

_____

People can't make me _____

_____

I am strong enough to _____

_____

▶

I'm not afraid to _____

_____

Something that I can do now that I couldn't do last year is _____

_____

I used to have difficulty dealing with _____

_____

but this is no longer a problem.

I have accomplished _____

_____

If I want to I can _____

_____

People like me because _____

_____

My greatest achievement is _____

_____

I have the courage to _____

_____

Note: this activity highlights some of the many talents you possess.
Concentrate on developing this list further.

 **activity**

Reviewing your achievements

Go back to the life line activity that you completed earlier and, in your log book or on paper, make a detailed list of all your achievements above the line under three headings:

● Personal

● Relational

● Career.

The next stage is to expand each achievement in a special way called 'FABing', which stands for:

● **Feature:** what did you actually do? Describe your achievement as factually as you can.

● **Analysis:** an achievement is not real if it cannot be measured in some way in terms of number, amount, percentage or value. This is not always easy but if it cannot be measured then either it is not a real achievement or you have used 'fat words' to describe it.

● **Benefit:** what was the actual advantage or benefit to yourself and what was the personal development that was gained from what you did?

For example:

Personal

● **Feature:** Made sports captain at school.

● **Analysis:** There were 53 boys in my year at school so I was first out of 53.

● **Benefit:** Developed my leadership, team and motivational skills.

Relational

● **Feature:** Developed my network.

● **Analysis:** Currently 176 people that I know and they know me. Joined Facebook and LinkedIn.

▶

- **Benefit:** I can always find someone to give me good advice on almost any subject. In the past, through my network, I was able to find my current job.

Career

- **Feature:** Streamlined the reconciliation process in the accounts unit at work.

- **Analysis:** Reduced 32% of the outstanding items and saved three days of labour hours.

- **Benefit:** Developed a reputation for improving processes which helped me gain the assistant manager position.

When failure strikes, as it always does when we are pushing the boundaries in life and work, we feel disappointed with ourselves, and thump self-confidence. Should this occur, then just take out and read your achievement list to yourself out loud. This will remind you of your successes in the three important areas of your life. When you do push the boundaries and you are successful then add that achievement to your list.

A wonderful psychological power of your achievement list is the sure and certain knowledge that you achieved those elements and no one can ever diminish or take them away from you.

 'Whatever we expect with confidence will be our own self-fulfilling prophecy.'

Brian Tracy, life coach

 'The way to develop self-confidence is to do the thing you fear.'

William Jennings Bryan, American politician

'You gain strength, courage and confidence by every experience in which you really stop to look fear in the face. You are able to say to yourself, "I have lived through this horror. I can take the next thing that comes along." You must do the thing you think you cannot do.'

Eleanor Roosevelt

brilliant recap

- We have examined what self-confidence is and why it's important – including the benefits of behaving with aplomb, assuredness and self-trust.

- Voices from our childhood and faulty thinking about our behaviour can dilute our self-confidence.

- We need to recognise and deal with the tyranny of 'must's', 'ought's' and 'should's'.

- We take notice of negative voices because they come from those who were emotionally significant to us when we were young.

- You can master the negative voice in such ways as naming the critics, reversing your thinking, getting a counter voice and focusing on your strengths.

CHAPTER 15

Achieving success out of failure

'Failure' – isn't it a terrible word? Like 'plague', 'death', 'redundancy' or being 'fired'. It sounds so absolute and debilitating. We live in a culture of excellence where success is everything. Winners win fame and fortune; losers get nothing. If the media is to be believed, winners are a race apart, each one a Midas turning everything they touch into gold. But the reality is we all have feet of clay and the world is fickle in its distribution of good fortune and loss. What is important is how you deal with failure. Successful people fail just as much as the rest of us, but the difference is how they regard failure, how they manage it and how they turn it into success.

Failure is essential to success

Failure is an essential component of success. It's not the intention of Mr Mistake and Ms Error to discourage you or make you give up and throw in the white towel. Their true motive is just to stop you in your tracks so that you can reassess your situation, learn the lesson being given and get on the road to success with more knowledge and experience than you ever had before.

Giving her speech at Harvard University in 2008, J.K. Rowling[1] of *Harry Potter* fame echoed these sentiments when she confessed:

---

1 *Harry Potter and the Philosopher's Stone* was mostly written in cafés because Rowling, recently divorced and totally broke, could not afford heating. In addition the book was rejected nine times before the publisher took the risk ... on an unknown.

'Failure gave me an inner security that I had never attained by passing examinations. Failure taught me things about myself that I could have learned no other way.'

Failure gives you the opportunity to re-strategise, and re-launch again to better prepare you for success. We learn more from the scar tissue we gain from the wounds of failure than the curriculum of any theoretical qualification.

You will recall that early on I suggested that failure in developing a new skill or competence failure is inevitable and goes with the territory. Remember the juggler's mantra:

'If you ain't dropping then you ain't juggling.'

Well, it applies not only to juggling but to life itself. Realistically, life itself is a series of successes and failures, and sometimes we can only get things right by getting them wrong. It is very easy never to fail – just do absolutely nothing. In fact, no failure results in no successes. We now know only people now who are not making mistakes or failing are those who have taken up permanent residence in a graveyard.

Many people don't try because trying and pushing the boundaries means the possibility of failure. When the fear of failure is dominant in a person then failure comes with a guarantee.

 'Failure is not falling down but refusing to get up.'

Chinese proverb

In Zen philosophy it is suggested that life is a series of lessons and if you ignore them then life repeats the lessons until you have learnt them.

T.S. Eliot, in one of his less enigmatic poems, gave us all quintessential advice by writing:

'We had the experience but missed the meaning.'

And this is the essence of making success out of failure. If you miss the meaning of your experience then you invite failure. All of us make mistakes but if we make the same mistake in the same situation, over and over again, then we have been missing the meaning. Of course failure hurts and is humbling. None of us sets out to fail at anything but sometimes it's inevitable, so let's turn to the question: 'How do we make success out of failure?'

Dealing with failure

It's important not to let your ego get in the way and push your mistakes into a deep hole where neither you nor others can find them. Admitting your mistakes and errors is the first rule of achieving success from your failures. You can't do anything about that which you pretend doesn't exist.

As already stated, neither you nor I set out to fail at what we do. We act with the knowledge and information we have available to us at the time. If this is so, how can we, when faced with failure, become disappointed with ourselves or our efforts? Hindsight always has the advantage of 20:20 vision and, if you had had 20:20 vision in the first place, you would have done things differently.

 'Failure is the crucible that tests your commitment, your courage and your moral fibre.'

Anon.

Managing failure requires resilience which is that 'getting back on the horse' phenomenon. Brush off the dust and climb back in the saddle knowing that sometime in the future life is going to buck you off again – you won't know when, or how or where, but the fact that you know that it is going to happen should not deter you, even when you find yourself on the ground yet again.

 **tip**

Success is never permanent and failure is never final.

Psychology and failure

One of the basic maxims of human psychology is very simple: 'We maximise pleasure and avoid pain'. On the basis that mistakes and errors are painful, then the obvious way of dealing with that pain is to avoid the same situation again. However, if you tread on your dancing partner's toes you will never be able to stop doing it if you sit out all the dances and look at your two left feet.

Successes from failures

This is the truth: you usually have to fail to succeed. Here are some global examples:

brilliant examples

1   Steve Jobs, at the age of 30, was fired from the company he co-founded. In his now famous speech at Stanford University in 2005 he said, 'What had been the focus of my entire adult life was gone, and it was devastating.' Then he went on to say, 'It turned out that getting fired from Apple was the best thing that could have ever happened to me … The heaviness of being successful was replaced by the lightness of being a beginner again, less sure about everything. It freed me to enter one of the most creative periods in my life.'

Jobs became involved in a small computer graphic company which became Pixar Animation Studios, which when sold made Jobs a billionaire. (Jobs unfortunately died in 2011.)

2 Akio Morita of Sony started out producing rice cookers – the only trouble was his product burnt more rice than it cooked.

3 Bill Gates' first foray into business was a disaster. His company Traf-o-Data processed paper tapes from traffic counters. When it was discovered that the product had many bugs, no local government would touch it.

---

 brilliant tip

No matter what the error is, the biggest failure is to let your emotions sabotage your journey.

'It's fine to celebrate success but it's more important to heed the lessons of failure.'

Bill Gates, founder of Microsoft

Strategy 1: do the analysis

Back to T.S. Eliot and 'missed the meaning'. You can ensure that this does not happen by asking some basic questions to max-imise your learning:

- What actually happened?
- Could I have seen the error earlier?
- Was the preparation adequate?
- Have I tried this before and failed?
- If so, why did I repeat my error?
- What alternatives did I consider?
- Were there enough resources?
- Was the objective reasonable?
- What was in my control?

- What was not in my control?
- What knowledge did I apply and was it adequate?
- What skills did I use and were they adequate?

Then come the two big and most important questions:

1 What did I learn?

2 What can I do differently next time?

With major errors and difficulties it is well worth writing down (in your development log book) what you have learnt and what you will do next time. In writing your learning points down you are far more likely to remember the objectives that you have set yourself.

Strategy 2: increase your risk-taking

This will increase your failures. This may sound counter-intuitive but it's effective because you are venturing into new fields and, as you do so, you are developing all the time. Obviously there are considerations here regarding how you perform in your job but remember that all the great entrepreneurs are risk-takers. Richard Branson's book *Screw It, Let's Do It*, personifies this risk-taking attitude.

Strategy 3: rejoice at failure

When we fail the usual response is negative: we might feel ashamed and we would certainly want to withdraw from those who know of our blunder. We feel that only success is worthy of celebration. However, given what we now know about failure and how it leads to our personal development, it's more appropriate to celebrate failure. The celebration of learning is a worthy activity. Negativity is limiting; positivity is liberating.

Strategy 4: find balance

When you have a string of successes, do not fall into the trap of thinking you will always have a charmed life. Similarly, if you have a run of failures this will not last. Somehow the world is like a flipped coin where, in the end, the number of heads equals the number of tails. If you think you are always going to win then when failure inevitably comes, and it will, you will be devastated and your recovery will take a long time. Similarly, if you have had a run of failure the danger is that you will give in and not try. Let me repeat myself: success is never permanent and failure is never final.

Strategy 5: examine what you learnt from your failures

Go back to the life line activity that you completed earlier. Where the line drops below average, see how it does not stay there but moves upwards towards an achievement. That indicates your personal learning and development. So list your failures in your log book and against each one record what you learnt and how you developed from that unfortunate experience.

Strategy 6: read biographies of the famous

This is most illuminating as one normally assumes that the famous go from strength to strength. Not so, and reading about your heroes and how they overcame adversity will not only inspire but will help you emulate their tactics and behaviour when things go pear-shaped for you.

Strategy 7: what is the worst that can happen?

So you fail: are you going to die, is your partner going to die? Of course not! Will your children still love you? Of course they will! These comparisons help put your failure into perspective and prevent you from 'dooms-daying'. Here is a true story:

 example

A friend of mine worked for a large event-management firm which was hired to provide catering for a very important event in the English social season. It involved hiring many casuals, tents and marquees, equipment, etc. My friend managed and co-ordinated all of this excellently. There was only one huge problem – he organised everything one week before the actual event. You can imagine not only the total chaos but the significant cost and implications for the company's reputation. The mistake was so enormous my friend was summoned to see the chairman to explain himself.

The result? He was not fired and in the years to come the chairman, with some devious amusement, would always ask his directors how my friend was doing.

I would not recommend this tactic but sometimes 'all's well that ends well'.

brilliant activity

Burn your errors

- Think about and list the major failures or errors in your life.
- Put each one a on a separate sheet of paper.
- Say to yourself, 'I did the best I could given my experience and my knowledge at that time.'
- Then say what it was that you learnt from the error.
- Having reflected on what you have learnt or how you have developed, put a lighted match to each piece of paper in turn and let them burn safely, one at a time, in a suitable bowl.
- As they burn, take a deep breath and then let any thoughts of self-inadequacy go.

'What the caterpillar calls the end of life, the master calls a butterfly.'

Richard Bach

 'The only real mistake is the one from which we learn nothing.'

John Enoch Powell, British politician

 brilliant recap

- Failure is essential to success; without failure there can be no learning.

- Mistakes, errors and failures cannot be avoided: they go with the territory of life.

- Admitting to failure is essential; you cannot learn if you don't admit to failure.

- Mastering failure needs the resilience not to give in and collapse but to get up and try again, and in the trying is the learning and self-development.

- There are seven strategies for the successful management of failure:

  1 Analyse what went wrong and what you need to do differently next time.

  2 Increase your risk-taking.

  3 Rejoice at failure.

  4 Find balance.

  5 Examine what you have learnt.

  6 Read biographies of the famous.

  7 Consider what is the worst that can happen.

CHAPTER 16

Achieving
assertiveness

Assertiveness is about being your true self, expecting to be treated properly by all and treating others in the same way. Being assertive usually falls into the realm of communicating with others, giving you the ability to be open, frank, honest and direct in what you say. In being assertive you take responsibility for your actions whilst respecting others and not judging them. Where there is conflict it provides the opportunity to be constructive and discover a win–win solution.

Assertiveness brings considerable advantages including, but not limited to, the following:

- It assists in the achievement of personal goals.
- It makes us feel good about ourselves and strengthens our self-esteem.
- It makes it so much easier to say what we want to say, irrespective of it being positive or negative.
- It prevents us from being taken advantage of by others.
- It diminishes our anxiety.
- It helps us make independent choices.
- It creates mutual respect with others.

All these advantages exist because the foundation of assertiveness is based on certain fundamental rights which accrue to us all. Basically this means that you can act in a way without having to justify yourself or your behaviour, and you would expect others to support you in the exercise of these rights. Unfortunately, if you are unable to exercise your rights then you become stressed and anxious. In addition you are likely to miss out on those things that you really would like to have or do, and this will impoverish your relations with others.

Your rights

So what are these rights that are so important? There are at least 10 of them:

1. You have the right to decide what you want to do with your life

It's up to you to set your own destiny and fulfil your ambitions in life. Fortunately, or unfortunately, you don't get the chance to go round again. This is important because if you don't set your own agenda you'll quickly find that you are working to someone else's. So you must do what *you* want. However, there is a corollary. If you choose to pursue a course in life, then you must also take the consequences of your decisions.

2. You have the right to express your views and opinions providing they are within the law

Your views about your situation or an issue are completely up to you and are just as valid as anyone else's. You might be wrong but you still have the right to express yourself and say what you wish even if you are in the minority that said 'The earth is round', 'Man will fly', 'slavery is not permissible.' You are also responsible for the response you get.

3. You have the right to be treated with respect

Because we live in a democratic and civilised society you have the right to be treated with respect and with courtesy, irrespective of your position or standing, in any situation.

4. You have the right to say 'No' or to refuse a request.

If you are serious about your self-development it will make demands on your time and consequently there will be occasions that, when others ask you to do something, in order to achieve your objectives you will just have to say 'No'.

Of course this does not mean you cannot say 'Yes', but what is important is that you are the person who chooses to give the affirmative or the negative response to a request. This may sound selfish but the fact is, the more you say 'Yes', the more people will begin to take advantage of you, and you may find that you have no time for yourself. In fact, you will have trained people to expect too much of you and when your breaking point comes, and you cannot do any more, you will not be thanked for all that you have done in the past, but challenged with 'Why have you let me down?'

5. You have the right to make mistakes

Much of the time in this world you get things right by getting them wrong first. Errors and mistakes lead to learning, just as much as getting it right first time. If we did not make mistakes today we might not have the advantage of vulcanised rubber for car tyres, stainless steel in our kitchens or saccharin in our tea.

6. You have the right to ask for what you want

We all have desires, wants and needs and if you don't ask, then you don't get. People don't have a crystal ball and intuitively know what you want or how to please you. In addition, by asking for what you want you will also help others to express themselves in the same way. So it's a basic right to ask for what you want. Of course there is no guarantee that you will receive what you ask for, but you are far more likely to get it if you ask.

7. You have the right to say 'I don't know'

How often have people challenged you by saying 'Don't you know that?' It's powerful to confess your ignorance and learn rather than feel inadequate. This is similar to the right to make mistakes in that you don't say or do things deliberately knowing that they are wrong or inadequate in some way.

8. You have the right to change your mind

If life is a process of learning then from time to time your opinion on things will change, sometimes quite considerably. After giving something some thought you might change your initial or original position. So when challenged with 'but you have changed your mind', inferring some inadequacy on your part, then it shows strength when you say 'Yes I have, because …'.

 'A mind that never changes is dead from the neck up.'

Father Max-Augustine

9. You have the right to decide whether or not to be assertive

Sometimes you will be happy to make accommodations for your children, your relatives and those who are important to you. What is critical here is that you are the person who decides how to treat the people in your life.

10. You have the right to be the judge of your own behaviour

If we are people of integrity, honesty and goodwill it's not appropriate for others to judge our behaviour – they may give feedback, but may not judge us in terms of right or wrong.

You don't need negative criticism from others to behave in the way that you wish. Your conscience will tell you when you err.

Additional rights

On reflecting on the above you may want to act as your own editor by deleting a right or adding another which is important to you. Here are some additional rights for you to consider. The right to:

- make your own decisions
- get involved in the affairs of others (or not)
- ask for more information when you don't understand
- say something which is illogical but which encapsulates your feelings
- state your limits and expectations
- obtain value for what you pay for
- do what you wish with your disposable income and/or leisure time.

If you wish to exercise your rights then two subsidiary articles go with your rights:

- First, you take responsibility for the outcome of your behaviour especially in exercising rights 2 and 4 above. Exercising number 2 could have significant implications for your career so perhaps there could be an underlying right: 'To ignore a right when the consequences would be too expensive.'
- Second, it is appropriate that you respect the rights of others. Life is a two-way street as far as rights are concerned.

Assertive behaviour

Now we have covered the important aspects of rights, we can move on to what behaviour we can expect from an assertive person. The assertive person can:

- refuse a request without feeling guilty

- control their feelings when under pressure
- ask for what they need without feeling guilty
- express their feelings to others without embarrassment
- make concessions to others out of choice rather than pressure.

The assertive person is able to:

- appreciate the views of others when contrary to their own
- disagree with someone without losing their respect or friendship
- support others when they are in difficulty.

Interestingly enough, if you examine the advantages of being dominant and the advantages of being non-assertive then you have captured the benefits of being assertive.

Here is how it works:

The advantages of each	
Being non-assertive	Being dominant
You don't always win	You have high self-esteem
You fit in easily	You get what you want
You don't feel guilty	You can express your needs
You don't upset people	You don't let people take advantage

So, in being assertive you gain the benefits of both dominance and being mild.

Let's now turn to the techniques/skills that accompany assertiveness and demonstrate how you can use these, too.

Asking for what you want

To be assertive you use the following structure:

- Use the person's name so that there can be no doubt as to who is to fulfil the request.
- Ask for what you want, being as specific as possible.
- Explain why you want it.
- Say when you want it by.
- Use the assumptive 'thank you'.

---

brilliant example

'Mary, I want you home at a reasonable hour tonight because I don't want you on the streets after the pubs close; so I expect you home by 10:45 pm. Thank you.'

Here the 'thank you' might seem a little strained but in fact it is very powerful because it assumes acceptance. When you say 'please' the initiative for compliance is transferred to the other person. A 'thank you' can also turn a request ('could you') into a command as in:

'Peter, could you do the stocktake today – thank you'.

Employing 'I' statements

'I' statements are incredibly powerful because they leave others in no doubt about who you are and what you need. 'I' statements enjoy the seal of assertiveness because they are factual, non-negotiable and describe the world as you see it. For example, should you say to someone: 'I have the feeling that you are not interested in my ideas', they will know exactly where you stand and how you feel. It cannot be disputed by the other person.

The statement 'I want your full co-operation' is far more powerful and urgent than 'Please will you co-operate.'

Combining 'I' statements

When you decide to be assertive then you put together a series of 'I' statements that cover:

- a factual assessment of the situation
- your interpretation of the situation as you see it
- how it makes you feel
- what you want in the future
- what will happen in the future if the situation is repeated.

 example

Factual assessment:

I see that this is the third time you have made that mistake even after extensive training.

Interpretation:

I have come to the conclusion that you just don't care.

Feelings:

I am very disappointed and surprised that you behave in this way.

Want:

So I want you to do this aspect of your work correctly.

Future action:

Because you are in your probationary period, I will have to let you go should this happen again.

The five 'I's in this example statement make it very powerful indeed, leaving the other person with no doubt about what is required and what will happen next if they don't comply.

Saying 'No'

If you are a helpful or passive person then your default position is to say yes when asked to do things. This can have the effect of training others to ask for your help, and they will expect you to respond positively. When you fail, because you just cannot cope, their response is not one of understanding but instead they feel let down. When your 'cup runneth over' with too much work or when you are asked to do something that you don't want to then you need to be able to say 'No'. Obviously if you just give a curt 'No' it's not going to help you in the popularity stakes, and if you use it on your boss it's not going to help you career aspirations. So the formula for saying 'No' assertively is as follows:

● Recognise the person by name.
● Use a softening statement to show that you understand what they want/need.
● State your position.
● With regret, say no on this occasion.
● If you wish, offer an alternative or a compromise.

---

brilliant example

'Look, Jack, I would love to do that for you and I recognise it's important for you to get it done, otherwise you would not have asked me in the first place. Now I just have to tell you that my current situation is this: on my to-do list I have abc, def, ghi, to get done by Friday and I just don't know how I am going to get to do jkl.

▶

So, regrettably, on this occasion I am going to have to say "No". If it still needs to be done then I might be able to help you next week.'

If it is your boss then you replace the last two sentences with something like:

'So please can you help me with a re-priority here because I certainly don't want to let you down.'

No promises that this will work but it's better than just saying 'No'.

Being assertive is more than just saying the words. It's important to exude confidence in a variety of ways since the way you deliver your message is just as important as what you say. Consider such things as:

- Your body language.[1] This must be congruent with your speech. This includes your shoulders being in parallel with the recipient's, your feet also pointing towards them and engaging in a high level of eye contact.
- Your voice. This needs to be firm as well as fluent, but not raised (which can show either anger or anxiety).
- When is the most appropriate time to make your statement.

Broken record

Children between the ages of three and eight use this assertive technique intuitively. All that is required is for you to repeat your request no matter what the justification is for not satisfying what you want. The posh name for this technique is 'repeated assertion' but 'broken record' describes it so much better. Employing it allows you to feel comfortable whilst ignoring the manipulative

---

1 For far greater explanation please see the sister book to this, *Brilliant Body Language* (2010).

negatives. This simple technique helps you to remain totally focused on what you want.

For example (said in a very firm but soft voice with a high level of eye contact – your lines are in italics):

'I would like to see the manager about the faults in this product that I purchased from you yesterday.'

'The manger is busy right now; can I help?'

'Thank you for being so kind but I want to see the manager.'

'If you have a complaint you must go to the complaints department on the third floor.'

'I know where that department is but I want to see the manager.'

'The manager will only tell you what I have said.'

'So he might, but I still want to see him.'

'But this is not our procedure.'

'It might not be but I want to see the manager.'

'Sir, this is getting very tiresome!'

'I'm sure it is, but I want to see the manager.'

And on and on until the other person gives in. Those of you who have had the pleasure of the company of a three-year-old daughter in a supermarket will know the eventual outcome when she says to you 'But, Daddy, I want that doll'!

Fogging

So often when we are criticised we become defensive, particularly if it's unjustified. Fogging provides a method for dealing with such a situation and uses whatever truth there is in the accusation to agree with the other person.

So, for example (the italics again are your response):

'You are so stupid.'

'You could be right, I'm not the sharpest knife in the box but I get along OK.'

'You will never be a success.'

'You could be right. We will just have to wait and see, won't we.'

'You're hopeless.'

'You're right, I'm not always successful but I do my best.'

Once you have agreed with the person, since no one is ever perfect in everything, the other person has nowhere to go with their criticism.

Negative enquiry

If you think that the criticism could be valid then it's important for you to gain specifics from that person and put an end to any manipulation, should there be any. Negative enquiry is very simple: you just ask for examples and more information.

For example:

'You are not very professional.'

'In what way am I not professional?'

'You're too scruffy.'

'Could you be more specific?'

'Well, your hair for a start.'

'In what way is my hair not professional?'

'It is far too long.'

'How does it being too long make me unprofessional?'

'Most people who are accountants have short hair.'

'So what you are really saying is that you have reservations about the length of my hair?'

'Yes.'

'Thank you. I will think about it. Is there anything else you would like to mention concerning my professionalism?'

And you go on in a similar vein until the other person cannot think of anything else. In my experience, once you have used this technique on a person who is trying to be manipulative they don't come at you again.

Where the other person is being sincere in their intent, this technique can deliver some very useful feedback and you will have learnt far more about yourself than if you had responded with aggression rather than being assertive.

Workable compromise

It's nearly impossible to always get your own way in life. Always look for a compromise and use the little word 'if', so that, should the other side not accept your offer, it can simply be withdrawn. Where you feel that your self-respect and/or values are being undermined then there can be no compromise and you should bring into play all your assertiveness skills.

Using assertiveness

Assertiveness is a useful communication tool. Its application is contextual and it's not appropriate to be assertive in all situations. Remember, your sudden use of assertiveness may be perceived as an act of aggression by others. In becoming assertive, may I suggest that you try it out on people that don't know you very well. As you become more skilled (practice makes perfect), you can introduce it slowly into your mainstream life and you will begin to gain all those benefits that we set down at the beginning of the chapter.

 **brilliant** recap

- Assertiveness enables you to achieve what you want whilst feeling good about yourself and enjoying freedom of choice and the respect of others.

- Understand your basic rights and give yourself permission to be who you want to be.

- Basic assertive skills include:

    - asking for what you want – if you don't ask you don't get

    - using 'I' statements – so people know exactly where you stand and what you want

    - saying 'No'.

- To prevent you taking on too much or being taken advantage of, use:

    - broken record – a powerful way of getting what you want

    - fogging – so you can't easily be manipulated

    - negative enquiry – so you can achieve precise feedback

    - workable compromise – so you get the best deal.

CHAPTER 17

Dealing with change

I t used to be death and taxes that you couldn't avoid but now, if you are breathing, expect change. No one so far has found a way to prevent change in themselves, in their families, in their friends, in their work or in their world. Change is endemic and here to stay. As we don't have a choice about it and it's unavoidable, the only possible thing that is negotiable is how we manage it.

Resisting change

As humans, once we have learnt to do something, even simple things, we become very suspicious of change and the older we are, the more resistant to change we become. Most people when confronted with change will say 'No', before they say 'Maybe', before they say 'Yes'. Change is not easy and we resist change for many reasons.

Our fears might include:

- fear of the unknown
- fear of failure
- fear of looking stupid.

Our possible losses could be:

- loss of status
- loss of friends and relationships
- loss of the familiar.

Our possible pain might be:

● the pain of losing friends and colleagues
● the pain of confusion and self-doubt
● the pain of family and peer-group pressure
● the pain of losing the past.

All the above factors, and many more, have an emotional impact because change brings about loss and grieving, with the major emotions and responses being:

● **Anger:** everything from whining to rage, often undirected or unfocused. This can lead to 'foot dragging', mistakes, poor interpersonal relations and even sabotage.
● **Bargaining:** unrealistic attempts to avoid the situation or make it go away, attempts to strike a special deal, or to work harder so it won't happen, etc.
● **Anxiety:** silent or expressed, this is a realistic fear of the unknown or simply catastrophic fantasies.
● **Sadness:** from silence to tears – the heart of the grieving process.
● **Disorientation:** confusion and forgetfulness and, even among organised people, a feeling of loss and insecurity.
● **Depression:** feeling of being down or flat, having the blues, a feeling of hopelessness and being tired all the time.

Dealing with the change situation

With all these negative emotions how do we deal with the change situation? Basically there are four ways in which we respond to change but only one of them (navigator) is helpful and healthy.

Victim

Here you are inert to the process and the problem that needs to be solved or the process that needs to be improved. The victim just suffers pain and is incapable of doing, or does not want to do, anything to relieve it. Victims become isolated as the initial situation develops and moves on. They are passed over and forgotten, like in a medieval battlefield, where the wounded were left to die, usually of gangrene. In organisational terms they are the first to be amputated from the company.

Bystander

Unlike the victim, who appears to suffer but does nothing, if you are a bystander you are totally passive and appear uninvolved and unaffected. You watch what is happening but take no action. You offer no support and no advice. You neither help nor hinder the process as you make your way to the sidelines of the activity.

Critic

Here you play the role of 'The Abominable No Man', standing high in the snow pointing out confusion when and wherever you can. Nothing can please you: everything is wrong with the vision, the process and the system. You are blind to any benefits in the end result. You enjoy a life membership of the 'even if it's broke don't change it' brigade, doing all you can to undermine progress.

Navigator

Here, you are being as constructive as you can, seeing opportunities, giving advice and being helpful wherever you can. You make a real effort to see the end result and provide suggestions as to how to arrive there.

Not all of us can be a navigator and for most of us it's normal and to a certain extent even healthy to experience grieving for that which is no more. If you know how your grief might manifest itself then, should it occur, you are in a stronger position to deal positively with your inner feelings. Below we discuss the more common emotions you may feel when you recognise that the change is inevitable and there is nothing you can do, except to do your best to manage it.

Change as a process

Change can be a single event in time but the emotional transition is a process that we have to work through. Most of us can only adapt slowly as the new situation occurs or unfolds. We cope with transformation by going through changes in our emotions and our behaviours. Adjustment to change can be experienced as a process with various elements and stages.

Although everyone is slightly different in how they deal with letting go of the old and accepting the new, we usually follow the stages outlined in the following diagram. Whilst it is time-based, the time you 'stay' in one stage varies significantly from person to person.

We can show this diagrammatically:

Disbelief

When the change first makes itself known a common reaction is disbelief. You say to yourself, 'This is not happening, this is so unexpected, this cannot be, etc.' Rather like the poor policeman who has to inform a mother that her boy has been in a fatal accident and gets the response, 'No, that's not my Johnny – you must be wrong.'

Emotional reaction

There are feelings of anger. You say to yourself, 'This is not fair, I don't deserve this, this shouldn't happen, I am going to see my solicitor, MP, shop steward, etc.' I can remember when I was 15 and working on a building site during my summer holiday. Work ran out and I was fired. To my later considerable embarrassment I told the foreman that he couldn't fire me … and anyway I was going to tell my Mum!

Fantasy

Here you try and escape the reality of the situation. You say to yourself, 'This might not happen, it's just a bad dream, someone is going to stop this, somehow the situation will be reversed, etc.' Once, in Scotland, I was working with some employees who had just been made redundant because their factory was closing. The employees were absolutely adamant that the business would be bought and they would keep their jobs. They still stuck to their position even when I pointed to the window which looked out onto the car park where lorries were taking away all the machinery from the plant.

Capitulation

This is perhaps the worst stage, when you know that the change is inevitable and you feel that you will not be able to cope with the new situation. You say to yourself, 'This is the end for me, I will never be able to cope, I might just as well give up, life has no meaning anymore, etc.' Unfortunately, one person in 5000, when they lose their job, choose suicide.

Self-reliance, growth in confidence, new skills

As the situation moves on, the individual discovers that they can adapt to the new situation and it's not as bad as they thought. It's almost as if they have discovered our mantra, 'If it's going to be, then it's down to me.' From the new situation they develop new skills and some of the experiences are, to their surprise, enjoyable. Things, ways and methods they thought were stupid and would never work actually have real benefits.

Rather than looking back to 'the good old days' they begin to look forward to what else the new situation will bring.

Integration and acceptance

This is the final stage; the individual has accepted their new situation as the norm. For them there is closure and the old situation is history; they have no more emotional lingering for it. They are totally 'at home' in the situation which, for them, is now normal.

The four basic survival rules for change

Should you find yourself, and I am sure you will, caught up in a change in your work or in your life here are some suggestions that will help you cope and come out on the other side:

- **Rule one:** recognise your resistance and emotions but force yourself to show up and be seen to be there. You have to be in it to win it.
- **Rule two:** let go of the past and live in the present. Don't just be there in body. Recognise that the change is real and that you are part of it. Tell the truth to yourself – don't compromise your integrity. Give it your best.

- **Rule three:** look after yourself physically and gather a support group. Stay away from negative people. Verbalise your difficulties, fears and hopes.

- **Rule four:** anticipate more changes. Realise that you cannot always get what you want. Give it your best shot and be satisfied. Leverage off your existing skills. Learn to do what you can do and let go of what you can't control.

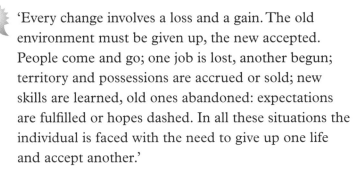

'Every change involves a loss and a gain. The old environment must be given up, the new accepted. People come and go; one job is lost, another begun; territory and possessions are accrued or sold; new skills are learned, old ones abandoned: expectations are fulfilled or hopes dashed. In all these situations the individual is faced with the need to give up one life and accept another.'

Colin Murray Parkes, author of *Bereavement: Studies of Grief in Adult Life*

brilliant tips

Managing change for your development

- Be very clear what is and what is not in your control. Only be concerned with that which you can control. Concern about the bigger picture only results in unwanted stress.

- Share your fears with someone you trust. We have already covered co-counselling and why it works. As you share your concerns and worries, strategies and options begin to manifest themselves.

- Work hard on options that are available to you. These are the 'if X ... then Y' opportunities.

- Use your network. Someone you know has gone through this change or something like it. How did they cope, what did they do and, more importantly, what did they learn? And how would they do it differently next time?

- All change is stressful so refresh some of the stress management techniques suggested in this text.

- Look after your body, eat sensibly, exercise and sleep eight hours a night. Change makes significant demands on your body and unless you are fit you will find that your immune system is considerably weakened.

- Remain flexible in your attitude and your outlook. If you stick in the past then you will miss the opportunities that life throws at you. You cannot develop your life by looking back all the time. As the saying goes: 'Fighter planes do not have a rear-view mirror.'

- Spend more time with your family and your friends. Clinging to your concerns and worries will damage the relationships that you value.

- If you are in control of the inevitable change then it is advisable not to rush. Baby steps are best, reviewing your progress as you go and learning from any errors. If possible, go for some early wins to provide encouragement and the motivation to continue.

 **brilliant** recap

- It's natural not to want to change the way we have always done something.

- There are lots of reasons why we don't like to change. These are to do with fear and the pain of loss.

- There are six negative emotions associated with change and basically four positions people take when confronted with change.

- We can understand change as a distinct emotional process moving through disbelief, an emotional reaction, fantasy, capitulation, self-resilience, new skills, developing confidence and finally integration and acceptance.

- There are nine points covering how to personally manage change successfully.

CHAPTER 18

Achieving relaxation (and reducing stress)

S
elf-development requires extra work and effort from you if you are going to succeed in achieving your aspiration to be the best you can be. It is no surprise, then, that as you take on more responsibilities there is the strong possibility that your stress levels will increase.

If you are stressed, personal development becomes 'the elephant in the room' – you know that you want to develop yourself but you just don't have the time or the energy to do it.

To assist you in dealing with this conundrum, this chapter will help you to manage your stress and achieve relaxation should things get too much (or indeed already be stressful) for you.

There are many different definitions of stress. Here is a common one:

 **brilliant** definition

Stress

Stress is a condition or feeling experienced when a person perceives that demands exceed the personal and social resources the individual is able to mobilise.[1]

---

1 Richard L. Lazarus (1999) *Stress and Emotion.*

Stress cannot be pushed aside or toughed out. It invades your subconscious through dreams and breeds concern, anxiety, apprehension, disquiet and foreboding. It used to be death and taxes that were the only certainties in life but today we can add stress as one of life's certainties. The list of stressors continues to expand and includes our children's development, finances, our relationship with our partner, family health issues, our parents' health, our own health, our in-laws and all the other curve balls that today's domestic life throws at us. Then there are work issues ...

One of the difficulties is that stress is cumulative, just like the proverbial camel with a maximum load capacity, and the ultimate straw. It can be just a minor issue that starts it and even happy events such as Christmas and birthdays can cause stress. As one cynic remarked, the reason mothers cry at weddings is just stress relief that the event is now over!

So stress acts like a slow drip from a tap and eventually fills a bucket and overflows. Drips of stress build up sometimes imperceptibly and then suddenly you fail to cope. Your immune system, having been weakened by this continual dripping, becomes unable to fight off something as minor as the common cold right through to something far more serious.

Because the dangers and benefits of stress management are so significant both at home and at work it is important we spend some time covering it.

As we can see from the diagram opposite, not all stress is bad for us. Without it most of us would be tuned out or sleepwalking. It is when we go into overload – physically, emotionally or socially – that we have problems coping and need to find ways to relax.

How much we can take before we go into overload and collapse is dependent on our personality, experience and circumstances, but everyone has a personal limit. After a charity event the posh Mrs Beckham, assisted by the famous David, was allegedly

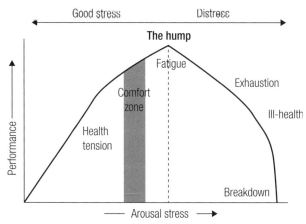

Source: Adapted from Nixon, P. (1979) *Practitioner*

heard to remark, 'Being famous ain't half hard.' No matter who you are, coping with the unexpected and the unwanted will be part of your life.

We have not changed from our cave-dwelling ancestors with regard to our reaction to perceived danger in that we fight, flee or freeze. Rarely, in our modern life, is any one of these three the best or most appropriate response, as exampled by road rage, running away from an accident or freezing up in a traffic jam. At our most stressful moments, our bodies respond with an increase in blood pressure and pulse rate, a rise in blood sugar and stacks of endorphins. This is a terrific, most useful response if you are being chased by a sabre-toothed tiger, but not if you are stuck in a car or you are being rousted in a work meeting.

Of course, the best thing to do in stressful situations is to remove yourself, but this is not advised if you have a high-powered job or a sudden domestic crisis which needs to be solved. Your body can only withstand so much continual stress before it decides that enough is enough, and then no matter what you think you can do, your body, independent of your conscious mind, says 'No' – this can be in a variety of ways, including impoverishing your physical and emotional health and affecting your relationships.

If you are in a stressful job, have you ever noticed that come Saturday your body gives you a headache, or that at the beginning of a holiday an illness you have ignored almost seems to say 'Now it's my turn', and you have to take to your bed?

One of the good things about stress management is that recognising that you are stressed is a significant part of the cure.

Stress questionnaire

How well do you manage stress? Do this quiz to see where you stand. For each statement tick (a), (b) or (c).

1   For you, stressful situations are easy to anticipate:

   (a) Sometimes

   (b) Always

   (c) Never

2   Your stress levels are affected by:

   (a) Emotions and thoughts

   (b) Both a and c

   (c) The way you respond to life

3   When things get difficult you:

   (a) Think of all the other things that could go wrong

   (b) Think how to resolve the difficulty

   (c) Think who might help you with it

4   You plan how you will respond to stressful situations:

   (a) Occasionally

   (b) Always

   (c) Never

5   You're in a traffic jam and someone drives past you in the bus lane to your left. You:

   (a) Take their number and report them to the police

(b) Are annoyed for two or three seconds

(c) Shout out an expletive

6   Your partner screams at you for something you have done. You:

(a) Tell them how they are not perfect either

(b) Hear them out and, if appropriate, say sorry

(c) Raise your voice and justify yourself

7   You exercise:

(a) Every weekend

(b) Most days

(c) Hardly ever

8   On her first date, you tell your daughter she must be home at a certain time but she comes home one hour late. You:

(a) Forbid her to see that young man again

(b) Tell her she is grounded for a month in a stern voice

(c) Show your anger and disappointment

Scoring:

Give yourself the following points: (a) = 2; (b) = 1; (c) = 3.

Your score: _____

Score 1 to 10:
Suggests that you are good at stress management. You can recognise stressful events as they arise and do your best to cope with them. If you like, you can skip this chapter.

Score 10 to 16:
Your stress management is not as strong as it could be. When you are beginning to feel stressed, stop and consider your options and how you might deal with the situation.

▶

> **Score 17 to 24:**
> You tend to bottle things up until you reach exploding point. Try talking about your worries before they get too big to handle. Make more time in your life for relaxation and develop some strategies to let off steam constructively.

Signs of stress

When something happens unexpectedly your body will go into fight-or-flight mode and this may include some or all of the following physical changes:

- your breathing increases
- you feel fatigue
- you experience headaches
- your heart rate increases
- your muscles become more tense
- you perspire more
- you get butterflies in your tummy
- you need to urinate.

This may assist you with the immediate situation if you are facing a physical threat but in today's environment this is rare. Consequently, with no outlet, if the situation continues the following symptoms begin to appear:

- impoverished decision making
- difficulty in concentration
- perceiving threats when there are none
- rise in moodiness
- increase in anxiety
- reduction in socialisation.

It gets worse because, should the situation become long-term then there is a strong likelihood of the following occurring:

- changes in appetite – eating more or less
- changes in sleep habits – too much or too little
- nervous tics begin – twitching, nail biting, teeth grinding, hair twiddling, pacing
- increase in minor illnesses – skin rashes, tummy aches and muscle pains
- impairment of sex life
- feeling constantly tired and worn out.

Recognising stress from changes in your behaviour

Recognising how stressed you are is not as easy as one might think. If you are one of life's procrastinators then it is not your work or you domestic life that is the problem but your procrastination. It's important to be honest with yourself: is it you that causes stress from your thoughts, your 'Doomsdaying' or your moods or attitudes towards life generally? If so, unless these change then stress is yours to keep.

Are you trying to escape stress by:

- aggressive behaviour without any justification
- drinking to excess
- being 'just busy' and ignoring the stressor
- isolating yourself
- pill popping
- excess computer gaming
- procrastinating
- smoking more
- watching too much TV
- eating too much or too little?

The benefits of stress management

By managing stress you can reduce the occurrence of any or all of the following:

- anxiety attacks
- high blood pressure
- chronic pain
- fatigue
- increased heart rate
- headaches
- insomnia
- irritable bowel
- muscle tension
- pre-menstrual syndrome (PMS)
- respiratory difficulties
- substance abuse.

This will, in turn, lead to an improvement in your sleep patterns, your sex life and your immune system.

The psychological benefits of managing stress include a reduction in:

- anxiety disorders
- depression
- eating disorders
- interpersonal conflict
- obsessive-compulsive disorder
- phobias.

Consequently there is mounting evidence that stress management can make you healthier and happier, and thus make self-development so much more easier and fun.

Managing stress

Just as individuals become stressed by different experiences so it is important to find what stress management techniques work for you. For instance, some people relieve their stress by jumping out of perfectly good aircraft at between 10000 and 14000 feet; they enjoy it hugely and call it sky diving. For the rest of us, I suspect the majority, it would send our blood pressure and our anxiety levels almost as high as the aircraft. Stress is idiographic – psychobabble for highly individual. Because of this individuality, what follows is a variety of stress reduction techniques. We will adapt that famous quote from Abraham Lincoln:

> 'Some will work on people most of the time, but they will not all work on all of the people all of the time.'

In other words, it's up to you, when you are stressed, to discover what works for *you*.

Specific coping strategies

Remove yourself

Just removing yourself from the stressful situation is by far the quickest, cheapest and most effective way of reducing stress. However, in the way that most of us live, such a solution is easy to say but difficult to do. It's not recommended to get out of your car when you are in a frustrating traffic jam and I certainly don't advise leaving your job unless you have a better and less stressful one to go to.

Learn to say 'No'

When your 'cup runneth over' you need to say 'No', otherwise you will definitely become stressed by trying and failing to keep up with your obligations. We learned how to say 'No' earlier (see Chapter 16).

Compromise

If you are a 'yes or no', 'black or white', 'my way or the high way' sort of person, life will not always allow you to get your own way and such situations can be stressful. Most times when people are being difficult it's not that they are difficult, it's just that they see the world differently to you. When you get to a roadblock ask yourself, 'Where are they coming from and how can I do a deal through a compromise that will still achieve a good outcome for me?'

What is the worst?

On a scale of 1 to 10 with 10 being the highest you have ever experienced, what would you score your present situation? The score is most probably less than 10, so you can say to yourself: ' I have managed situations worse than this situation I am currently facing so I have the skills and experience to deal with it.'

What is the gift?

In most stressful situations there are always benefits: we learn more, something occurs to our advantage, we grow in confidence or get applauded for our work. By concentrating on the gift this helps us deal with the stress of the moment.

Salami

One never eats all the salami at once but at a slice at a time. Treat the stress situation like a huge salami sausage and then break it down into thin slices and deal with them a slice at a time.

Surrender

There is a great little poem (which we met in an earlier chapter) that goes:

*'He who fights and runs away
Lives to fight another day.'*

What is important here is that it is you who chooses to surrender and it will be you who chooses to fight again, i.e. the stress does not defeat you and you remain in control.

Acceptance

This is very similar to surrender, mentioned above, but essentially it is a recognition that you do not control everything in your world. The advice here is more eloquently expressed in Reinhold Neibuhr's famous 'Serenity Prayer':

'God, grant me the serenity
to accept the things I cannot change,
and the wisdom to know the difference.'

Co-counselling

This requires a colleague who is prepared to say nothing but just listen to you as you verbalise your stressful situation and your anxieties. In explaining your stress to another person you have to give it a structure so that they can understand and, strangely, in that process you discover ways of coping with the situation. The stress is no longer just 'felt' but it has a logical structure. From there you can begin to demolish the structure.

Sport and exercise

Playing hard at any sport or giving your all in exercise will release all those endorphins into your body and give you that 'high' which will ameliorate the stress as well as preventing you thinking about the stressful situation. It's important to ensure that your exercise is fun – you don't want to add to your stress!

Listen to music

Listening to appropriate music, Mozart is top of the pops for this, reduces heart pressure due to stress. This is one of the reasons why many dentists now provide headphones during procedures.

It's important to have your favourite music as long as it is slow, as this will slow your thoughts down. If possible, slow your breathing to match the rhythm of the music and choose instrumental music rather than songs because the latter make you think when really you should just relax.

Use perspective

Most stress is locked in the here and now or the very near future. Gaining perspective is looking at the bigger picture. How does the now fit into the future, say in six weeks' time? Placed in this sort of perspective the stressor will more than likely shrink to its correct size in the grand scheme of things.

Group discussion

It provides a great relief to discuss your situation with others who are facing the same stressful situations. You are not alone and you can gain relief from others who have progressed further in dealing with their stress.

Deep breathing

The key here is to breathe from as low down in your tummy (abdomen) as possible thus gaining as much fresh air as possible. The more oxygen you can take in, the less stress you will feel. Inhale through your nose and exhale from your mouth, getting rid of as much air as possible. Once you are able to do this then breathe in threes: breathe in for three, hold for three and exhale for three. Doing this, you will find that your body begins to relax and communicates to your mind that all is well and all will be well.

You can get more sophisticated: as you breathe in think of all the cleansing, cool, fresh air you are taking in and as you exhale, breathe out all the things that are stressing you. It is a wonderful exercise.

Yoga and tai chi

These activities are great to achieve relaxation and gain a state of calmness and muscle easing. They also provide improvement in mood and enable you to focus away from the stressful situation.

However, both these systems of relaxation require regular practice and it's important to begin in a class where there are low physical demands placed upon your body, otherwise your physical pain will add to your stress!

Meditation

Meditation is a bit of a paradox because you can meditate by thinking on a particular subject and you can also meditate by doing the opposite, i.e. by not thinking. Consequently, as you can imagine, there are many definitions so here are some:

- Meditation is effortless concentration.
- Meditation is simply witnessing your mind without any involvement at all.
- Prayer is when you speak ... meditation is when you listen.

So if you are not already confused here is something from a Zen master:

- Meditation is to be intimate with all things.

To define meditation is like trying to describe to another person what a jelly fish looks like; you know it when you see it but it is almost impossible to describe. For meditation, you know it when you do it but it's difficult to describe.

Besides the more traditional Christian and Eastern methods, many new, perhaps alternative, forms have been developed, including but not limited to:

- bath meditation

- body scan meditation
- walking meditation
- mindfulness meditation
- music meditation
- kind thought meditation
- and even, a growing favourite, chocolate meditation!

This is not the place to teach you how to meditate but I do confirm absolutely that it will reduce your stress levels. There should be a good meditation centre in your nearest town.

Postpone

This is for minor, everyday stresses and it will stretch your credulity but please don't knock it until you have tried it! When the stressor comes – 'Will my daughter come home from her date by 11:00pm?', 'Will my presentation go well next week?', 'Will people enjoy themselves at my dinner party?' – then all you say to yourself, as soon as the worry occurs, is 'I just don't have time to worry about this. I will give myself all of five minutes to worry after dinner when I get home.' Give yourself that window to worry every day and most likely in the evening you will just forget to worry! Even if this doesn't happen the minor worry won't affect your current behaviour or performance.

Humour

It's no joke, humour really does reduce stress.[2] It's one of the fastest ways of reducing stress mainly because it forces your brain to think in a different way. It diverts your thoughts away from the stressor, shuts off the fight-or-flight hormones and so diffuses the stressful feelings. Humour works because laughter produces

---

2 Narula, R., and Chaudhary, V., and Narula, K., and Narayan, R. (2011) *Depression, Anxiety and Stress Reduction in Medical Education: Humour as an Intervention, OJHAS,* Vol. 10(1).

helpful chemicals in the brain such as gamma-interferon and T and B cells essential for our immune system.

What is really interesting is how there are cross-connections between humour and exercise. Laughing 100 times is equal to a 15-minute bike ride. One of the reasons why it is easier to sleep after watching a comedy is because when we laugh we give a great workout to our abs, back muscles, our diaphragm, breathing and, of course, our face muscles.

Hypnosis

Hypnosis can be used for stress management in two ways. First, it is like meditation in that it places you in a state of deep relaxation, and secondly, post-hypnosis suggestion can alter the way you think about a stressor. Such suggestions can also have a limiting effect on stress-induced behaviour including negative habits such as over-eating, excessive smoking and insomnia.

Sex

Here we save the most popular till last. Sex and love making are fantastic stress destroyers brought about by the huge incursion of endorphins that result from physical and emotional bonding. We have already mentioned that sometimes stress actually reduces the libido so it's difficult to 'get in the mood'. Perhaps trying some of the above methods first will help with this.

My best advice is to just start going through the motions, and you will be amazed how your body takes over.

 **brilliant** recap

- Stress reduction is very important for self-development because if you are stressed then self-development is put on the 'back burner'.

- If you are committed to self-development and you ignore it then this becomes an additional stressor.

- Stress is cumulative; a straw is a small thing but as it can break a camel's back so it can push you over the edge.

- You need to recognise good stress from bad stress – and ensure you don't move from rust-out to burn-out.

- The three responses to stress are fight, flight or freeze.

- There are physical and emotional signs of stress and these can be short- or long-term.

- We have learned how to recognise when you are stressed and discussed the physical and psychological ways of dealing with it.

- Stress management is highly individual – one person's stress is another's relaxation.

- Finally, there are 18 stress reduction techniques in this chapter for you to choose from.

PART 3

Understanding people

was once invited to write a piece for a finance magazine on the common attributes of Australia's richest. Of course there was not much that was common to these individuals but what was evident, besides their determination and not understanding the word 'can't', was the fact that most of them could be charming. Notice that I used the word 'could'. As a professional psychologist I was surprised by how quickly they sized me up, worked at my level and were pleasant and charming. So, in addition to all those aspects and attributes that go with success, they could quickly understand other people.

Since so many of the 'richest' share this competence it does suggest that to be successful is not only to know and challenge yourself but also to understand others.

In this, the final part of the text, we move from ourselves to others. It is trite, but right, that: 'We get by with a little help from our friends.'

So here we explore some ways which will help. Being a psychologist I fall back on psychometrics, which is always helpful in this area, then we move on to rapport skills and conclude with body language. In mastering these skills you should be able to get on with 97.5% of people. (The other 2.5% is the estimated number of people who unfortunately are chronically ill in ways which severely impoverish their life skills.)

CHAPTER 19

Understanding
other people

'Treat others as you would treat yourself' is a fine sentiment, for we would all like to be treated with kindness, respect and generosity. However, at a deeper level, this golden rule needs to have several corollaries because we are not all the same. Whether we are male, female, short, tall, introvert, extrovert, we are all absolutely unique. Even identical twins brought up in exactly the same way are not 100% identical.

It is this real individuality that brings with it both joys and difficulties, and presents a multitude of challenges when we try to work with and understand other people, particularly in the areas of influence and persuasion. For example, supposing someone's disposition is kind and helpful, and their default position is being accommodating and supportive, then one of the ways to approach them for help with your career, after an initial rapport discussion, would go something like this:

'I'm doing some work on myself to develop new competences so I can have a shot at a promotion – but I've hit a bit of a roadblock. I'd really like to talk through what I am doing, get some feedback and even advice. I wonder if you would be kind enough to be my mentor and help me though the process?'

Somehow I don't think this approach would work with someone who is highly individualistic, competitive and hungry for power. This person would probably be more influenced by a more direct approach with the possibility to shine as a result of assisting you, with a pinch of competition thrown in. One of the better approaches, after the initial rapport discussion, would go something like this:

'Doug in HR has suggested that I approach Sam Pringle to mentor me. I'm not sure if mentoring is something you generally do, but I'd really prefer to work with you – you have a excellent reputation for getting things done and I like your direct style. It is a big ask, but the CEO is very keen for people like myself to develop ourselves as much as possible and I'm sure he would take an interest. Please don't feel obliged as I could approach Sam, as suggested, but, in confidence, I feel you would be the better person.'

The way that I have phrased these requests may not be your style, but what is obvious is that both approaches have taken into consideration the individual, their disposition and personal style. So we are turning the original maxim on it head: your approach is more likely to be successful if you abide by the rule:

 'Treat other people as they would like to be treated.'

Then they are more likely to be persuaded. If this doesn't work then here are some basic maxims with which to play. First of all:

 'The more you do of what you're doing, the more you get of what you've got.'

If what you're doing is not working then the second maxim comes into play:

 'If what you are doing is not working then do something different.'

The third maxim is this:

 'The person with the greatest flexibility will win in every interpersonal situation.'

If this does not sound credible then think of very young babies. When they want something they smile, babble, cry, scream, hold their breath, go blue, defecate, kick their legs, wave their arms until they get what they want. Why? It's as if they are already familiar with and use the third maxim to communicate and control two adults to get what they want.

Discovering the difference in people

As an analogy, think of sports people: for example, David Beckham, the footballer, and Rebecca Adlington, the Olympic swimmer. These tremendous athletes enjoy the right body shape for their sport. All of us have personality 'shapes' and this becomes very important when we need to persuade an individual to do something. The best indicator of future behaviour is past behaviour, so even just thinking about a person's behaviour in the past will help you in your day-to-day interactions with them.

The MBTI

Perhaps the most widely used tool to illustrate how we are different is based on the work of Carl Jung. Essentially it is a four-by-four matrix system (interestingly not developed by psychologists but by an anthropologist and her daughter). The questionnaire is known as the Myers-Briggs Type Indicator® or MBTI. What is so powerful about this instrument is that the 4×4 matrix suggests that there are 16 different personality types. This might sound complex at first but once you have grasped the basics it becomes obvious.

The MBTI structure asserts that we are all either:

- Extrovert or Introvert
- Intuitive or Sensor
- Thinker or Feeler
- Judger or Perceiver.

To give you a flavour of the system, we will look at just two of those categories (Thinkers and Feelers, and Judgers and Perceivers) using the examples of how people make decisions and, by extension, how they like to be persuaded.

Thinkers (T) and Feelers (F)

Thinkers are logical, analytical and firm minded. In other words they use their heads to make most of their decisions. Some people known as 'Feelers' prefer to use another strategy when faced with a decision and are more comfortable using their heart and/or their value system to come to a conclusion. By and large their decisions are more humane, empathetic and tender hearted.

Judgers (J) and Perceivers (P)

Judgers tend to be controlled, disciplined and organised in their lives. Perceivers are more spontaneous and free spirited – preferring to wait and see what the future brings before making a decision, which to them is far more appealing than having a firm plan of operation. Judgers like closure and completion so that they can move on whereas Perceivers like decisions made as late as possible in case there is a new circumstance or opportunity just around the corner.

As you can see, should an extreme TJ person treat someone with an extreme FP personality in the same way that they themselves like to be influenced and persuaded, they will be like two ships passing each other at night in deep fog with neither vessel having the advantage of semaphore let alone radar. Logical, factual and realistic, the TJ person will bombard the FP person with logic in an effort to persuade them and will be surprised that their best efforts are to no avail, no matter how much they cry 'How can't you see! It is so logical! We have to do it this way!' Maybe if they had said 'How do you feel about this? Isn't it just right for this occasion? But hey, I don't want to rush you, tell me how you feel about it in the morning', they would have been more successful. Here we take a more emotional stance and give the other person time to consider all their options, leaving things open until the last nanosecond.

Important note: psychological boxes of people's personalities just go some way to helping us understand someone, but it's very important to remember that an individual is too unique to be caged in one of 16 boxes. We are all individuals and like no other person on earth either living or dead. These boxes are convenient but they are only constructs, not reality.

---

brilliant example

Many years ago I was invited by a major retail company to help the board of directors work better together and act like a cohesive team. The problem was easy to identify in that there were two categories of board member: those who had come up through the ranks (mostly 'Ps') and those who were professionals with lots of qualifications (mostly 'Ts'). One director, who joined the organisation as a sales assistant and worked his way up to being a director, went to the heart of the problem, telling me in no uncertain terms: 'Look mate, a brilliant retailer is someone who hasn't got an MBA and can sell stuff.'

You can use your imagination about the views his qualified colleagues (who were all 'Ts'), who had MBAs but had spent no time on the retail floor, held about him!

Examining differences

To be successful in life, it's important to get on with other people. Unfortunately, not everyone is easy to deal with and some individuals can be exceptionally difficult. One of the reasons why you perceive them as difficult is that you have not taken the time to understand them. You may remember from the musical *My Fair Lady* that Professor Henry Higgins get so frustrated with the flower girl Eliza Doolittle that he shouts at his colleague Colonel Pickering, 'Why can't a woman be more like a man?' Like most of us, the Professor expects everyone to have the same approach to others as he has. But of course this is impossible, since we are all so different one from another.

An easy way of understanding other people is simply to take some time to watch and listen, particularly when you are having difficulties with someone. But before you do this, spend some time reflecting on your own disposition and personality. Check out your thoughts with someone who knows you well. This will help you discover how you are different from other people and they from you.

brilliant tip

It would be to your advantage to swat up on the MBTI. Spend half an hour or so reading some of the excellent summaries of the work of Katharine Cook Briggs and her daughter Isabel Briggs Myers on the internet. Just Google MBTI and consider where your personality lies in the matrix.

Think about someone who you have difficulties communicating with. You have already noticed that their behaviour and preferences are different to yours so the next stage is to discover what drives their behaviour. Remember they are not being deliberately difficult, they just march to a different drum and you need to discover their beat.

It's also important to recognise your hot buttons and triggers: what is it about this person that 'gets under your skin'? Once you understand these triggers and what makes the other person 'tick' you're pretty much there in terms of communicating better with them and overcoming your differences.

'When we lose the right to be different, we lose the privilege to be free.'

Charles Evans Hughes, American statesman, lawyer and Republican politician

'If we are to live together in peace, we must come to know each other better.'

Lyndon Johnson, 36th US President

 **activity**

Questions to understand another person

Choose someone you find challenging to communicate with and work through the questions below. You might not be able to answer all of them but the process will certainly help you towards a better understanding of them and should improve your relationship.

1 What is it about this person that I like?

2 What is it about this person that I dislike?

3 What do I know about this person from their past behaviour?

4 What could be their Myers-Briggs® type personality?

5 What are their likes and dislikes?

6 How are they different from me?

7 What do I like about them as an individual? Why?

▶

8   What do I dislike about them as an individual? Why?

9   What do we agree about?

10   What do we disagree about?

11   What do they appear to believe in?

12   What are their values?

13   What three adjectives would describe this person?

14   What evidence do I have for this?

Now you have this information, how might you work differently with them in the future?

1   _____

2   _____

3   _____

4   _____

5   _____

 brilliant recap

- We are all different and unique.

- We need to be flexible and adapt to differences in others.

- The Myers-Briggs matrix helps us discover and understand differences in other people and ourselves.

- Identifying our 'hot buttons' allows us to stay in control and communicate better with others.

CHAPTER 20

Body language and rapport

Our ancestors hunted in groups, set up homes, decided when to move on and agreed who was the leader of the close family grouping, most probably through body language and signs. Speech, which was far more efficient for daily living, then developed and gradually our fluency in body language declined. We might not be as body-lingual as they were but much of that language is hardwired and we, without being conscious of it, still 'speak' it. Often it reappears in the form of intuition with such statements as: 'Strange, but there is something about that person I really like' or 'I can't say for sure but I don't think he is telling the truth.' What is being picked up here is what the other person's body is 'saying'.

Our body says all sorts of things, including but not limited to:

- I am anxious/confident.
- I am frightened/relaxed.
- I am pleased/disappointed.
- I am lying/telling the truth.

What is interesting is that our bodies start 'talking' way before the words come out of our mouths. We will perspire from anxiety, when public speaking for instance, long before we are conscious that we are sweating.

Reading bodies

When reading someone's body there are three very important things to keep in mind.

First, our bodies communicate in clusters of signs. Just because I touch my mouth doesn't mean I'm about to tell a lie as it could be just an itch that I need to scratch. But if other body signs occur at the same time, such as:

- perspiration appears
- speech slows up
- eye contact is lost
- a half smile is perceived,

then it would be reasonably safe to assume that what is about to be said needs to be verified before being accepted.

Second, context is also important. Let's take perspiration and add a dry mouth, which again might be a sign of mendacity, but if the room is hot and the person has just arrived in from the cold then this is more likely to be the body adjusting itself to the different environment. However, should perspiration suddenly occur for the first time in an interview candidate then whatever they say needs more probing as they may not be telling the truth.

Third is to do with sudden changes in the body. If we are sitting comfortably in a chair why would we suddenly move either forward or back from the person to whom we are talking? It could be discomfort but if it's sudden then it's more likely to be interest when we move forward and dislike when we move back.

My companion book *Brilliant Body Language* goes into far more detail on these matters so here we will just deal with the major aspects of body language that will be useful and relevant to self-development.

Your smile

If you wish to get on in all aspects of life, to relate well to others, to persuade and to get into a rapport quickly, then your smile is the best piece of equipment you have available to be proficient and successful in your relationships.

People can very easily detect a false smile where just your mouth and lower face go through the motions. In the full smile, technically known as a 'Duchenne smile', the whole face bursts into life. Your face crinkles, showing your crows' feet, and your eyebrows are slightly raised. In a really genuine smile the head also moves back slightly as if you are going to laugh.

When you use the full smile you will find that meeting someone, especially for the first time, goes particularly well, as does showing appreciation and acknowledging success.

A full smile indicates that you are not a threat, that you have great interpersonal skills and, although not true, is thought to indicate that you are more intelligent.

Your handshake

Most people are surprised to learn that there is no correlation between strength of a person's grip and the forcefulness of their personality. However this myth is so well embedded into popular psychology that it's an important aspect of self-development to be able to give a 'good' handshake. In your journey of self-development you are going to meet and work with many, many people and a firm handshake is going to create initial positive assumptions about you.

Here is how to do it:

● Hold your hand/palm vertically as in a karate chop, with your thumb up and your arm pushing your hand at elbow height towards the perimeter of your personal space.

- Make full palm contact with the other person and curl your thumb to make a grip. Their hand should be mirroring yours.

- As your hands lock, establish eye contact together with a full smile.

- As you do this your hands move up and down vertically about 10 centimetres twice. Release your hand and eye contact, and move back slightly letting your arm hang loosely by your side.

- If you wish to show respect or defer to the other person then nod your head slightly.

What not to do:

- Compete on who has the strongest grip.

- Play politician and turn your hand to the left so that it is on top or with your left hand grasp the other person's upper arm. Both movements indicate that you are going to be the top dog in the coming relationship.

- Wipe your hand on your side as if it now carries something contagious which has to be swabbed off.

- Males should not prolong physical contact with the other person if they find them physically attractive.

- Females should not 'dip' their eyes as in certain circumstances it can be taken to indicate availability.

The 75 body language signs[1]

It's impossible to cover in detail all the possible body language signs as this would take a whole book in its own right. Taken from the companion text to this, *Brilliant Body Language*, the following, in alphabetical order is a list of most of these signs

1 Based on the initial work of my friend Gabrielle Griffin and published in my companion text *Brilliant Body Language*.

with a brief explanation. Being able to recognise just some of those signs whilst engaging in conversation with others will be of tremendous benefit to your self-development since your communication, comprehension and rapport skills will be greatly enhanced.

Physical sign	Possible meaning
Adam's apple bobbing	Anxiety, lying
Arms crossed – one holding the other	Feels insecure
Arms in front of body, touching or holding handbag, jewellery, shirt cuff, etc.	Feels insecure
Arms and palms open	Open, honest
Arms crossed on chest	Putting a barrier between someone or something they do not accept thus showing a negative attitude
Arms holding handbag, cup (etc.) as a barrier	Feels insecure
Arms and hands in the 'Adam position'	Feels insecure
Blading (turning towards the other person so less of you is exposed)	Wanting to protect oneself
Blinking (increased)	Indication of anxiety
Breathing in deeply	Relaxation, acceptance
Chin stroking	Making a decision, evaluating
Duchenne smile	Welcoming, wanting to be friends, approval
Eyes glaze	Disinterest, thinking
Eye rubbing	Confusion, tiredness
Face-touching, including mouth, eyes, ears, neck	Concealing the truth or nervousness
Foot-pointing	Foot points in direction of attention (e.g. at door if person wants to leave or to someone they find attractive)
Fingers (or glasses, etc.) in mouth	Evaluation or needs reassurance

Physical sign	Possible meaning
Foot tapping	Boredom
Grooming self	Showing interest in another
Grooming another	Desiring to be intimate
Hand chopping	Aggressive emphasis
Hand gripping wrist with arms behind back	Total confidence or frustration and attempting self-control (the higher the arm grip, the higher the frustration or anger)
Hand resting against head	Interested evaluation
Hand slapping back of neck	Feeling threatened or angry
Hands supporting	Expressing power through using space
Hands clenched	Frustration (the higher frustration, the higher the hands)
Hands open and palms up	Submission
Hands – both supporting the face, face on flat hands	A feminine action to look attractive to attract a man's attention
Hands – holding behind back	Confident, authoritative
Hands in pockets	To look casual, to say 'impress me' or the person does not want to participate
Hands – rubbing palms together	Positive expectation
Hands – steeple, tips of fingers touching	Confident, relaxed, self-assured
Handshake: elbow grasp	An attempt at power, showing intimacy of friendship
Handshake: palm down	An attempt at power and control
Handshake: palm up	Giving the other person control
Handshake: shoulder hold	An attempt at power, shows close intimacy
Handshake: upper-arm grip	An attempt at power
Handshake: vertical palms and similar pressure	Shows respect, recognises equality and encourages rapport

Physical sign	Possible meaning
Handshake: wrist hold	Acceptable when two people are close
Hands-on-hips	Using space to show dominance
Hand-to-face gestures, all	Negative attitude, lying or nervousness
Hyperventilating	Fear, anxiety
Leaning forward	Interest, acceptance
Legs crossed	Closed, submissive or defensive attitude; in women it shows comfort
Legs in figure four cross – one foot resting on other knee	Confidence, dominant, competitive attitude
Legs open	Openness or dominance
Legs spread – amongst men	Use of space to establish authority
Lip biting	Anxiety, holding back a comment
Lip licking	Anxiety, attraction
Looking at watch	Wish to get away, boredom, inattention
Mirroring	Being in rapport
Mouth covering	Wanting to ask a question, about to lie
Movement forward	Interest
Movement backwards	Disagreement or anxiety
Palm closed and pointed finger	Anger to achieve submission or agreement
Palm down	Projecting authority
Palm up	Acceptance, readiness to listen
Preening	Wanting to be or being attractive
Quick/sharp intake of breath	Surprise, shock
Seating position – chairs directly opposite	Competitive, defensive position
Seating position – chairs side-by side on inward angles	Co-operative position

▶

Physical sign	Possible meaning
Smiling	Welcoming, non-threatening, asking to be accepted
Smile lower face only	Submission, insincerity
Smirk	Arrogance, insincerity
Speech fluent and fast	Enthusiasm
Speech suddenly slow	Lying
Standing tall	Wishing to dominate, to appear attractive, to control
Teeth clenched	Frustration, anger
Thumb – displays, often protruding from hands in jacket or trouser pockets	Superiority, dominance, striking a pose of authority
Thumbs tucked into belt/pocket	Sexually aggressive attitude
Tic, increased use of	Anxiety
Touching self	Anxiety
Turning away	Wishing to terminate the conversation

Making the connection: getting into rapport[2]

Natural rapport is really a subcomponent of body language. It's something we do if we like the person we are with. It can almost be summed up in two words – 'unintentional imitation' – because we get into rapport without thinking. Like breathing, for most of the time we do not even think about it – we just do it. If there are specific people we want to make a good impression on that we don't know yet, deliberately getting into rapport, whilst seeming a little Machiavellian, is a useful skill.

We have already covered the smile and the handshake, which will be a great start, but what comes next?

2 Pioneers in this work are Richard Bandler and John Grinder of NLP fame.

Mirroring

Next time you are in a social gathering or in a restaurant, observe the body positions of couples and you will see something quite interesting: people sitting opposite each other are almost a mirror image of one another. What is more interesting is that a dance is going on: when one person moves, soon after the other person moves in the same way, as if they are in a dance. Hands position themselves in the same way, as do arms, as do the shoulders, arms and feet. Heads nod almost at the same time. If one takes a sip of their drink, soon after the other person does the same.

So here is the first rule of engaging in rapport: make your body slowly move into an identical image of the other person's body language. This takes real skill and demands a lot of practice until you do it almost unconsciously, which you would do anyway if you really 'connected' with the other person. It's very important to be skilled at mirroring as no one likes to be mimicked. If someone knows about mirroring and sees your incompetent attempts at the skill they can have a lot of fun with you, moving, counter moving and employing strange positions just to see you trying desperately to catch up until you realise what is happening.

When you think that you have achieved rapport the next thing is to confirm it, and to make this assurance we have to engage in leading.

Leading

This is an important skill, especially when we want to persuade or influence someone, because we are more likely to be convinced by a person who is like us. We trust people who are like us.

This is how it works when you reverse roles. Up until now you have been following your partner to get into rapport, now it's your turn to move, cross your legs, alter the position of your arms – whatever. Then if the other person moves in the same way and mirrors you, you can be fairly confident that you have established rapport with that person. Now is the time to present your ideas or concepts, or offer a product or service that you want the other person to accept.

This, then, is the process:

Mirror   Establish rapport   Pace   Lead   They follow   Move to influencing

If the other person does not follow, then return to mirroring and repeat the cycle until they follow.

Master these skills, including how to introduce yourself effectively (which is covered in the following chapter), and you will be well able to build instant rapport and influence with anyone you meet.

 **brilliant** recap

- We speak more honestly with our bodies than we do with our words.
- We can learn how to read body moves and interpret them accurately.
- This must be done in the context of the social situation.
- Smiles and handshakes - you need to know how to do them properly so you are not disadvantaged.
- You now know 75 body language signs and what they could mean.
- We have learned how to confirm that you are in rapport with the other person and when it's appropriate to attempt to persuade them.

CHAPTER 21

Building your network

When we lived in a cave we lived with our extended families, when we came out of our caves we lived within our tribe, then it was village life and most of our life was spent with others within a 20-mile radius (the distance a reasonably fit horse could make a return journey in a day). Then something happened, there were more and more of us and less and less in terms of our contact time with our direct family – have you counted recently the distances between your direct family members? With my brother in Ibiza, one sister in Devon and the other in Kent, my children in Sussex and my wife and I living in the suburb of Bondi Beach down under, you can imagine we don't get together too often.

For most of us, our lifestyle can be summed up in one word – 'isolationist'. The average person watches television for 18 hours a week. A highly individual activity since we only talk during the commercials. Often the children are stuck in front of other screens, we all live in houses with fences around them, travel to work on our own in the car or in trains, putting on a face that dares anybody to speak to us.

Have you ever noticed that walking in a city you don't greet people but if you were on a lonely country path and someone was coming in the opposite direction you would? Oh, of course we have mobiles, emails and the whole of the social media world to communicate with, but that's not the same as establishing and maintaining an interpersonal relationship.

The words of the Dalai Lama express this concept beautifully:

'We humans are social beings. We come into the world as a result of others' actions. We survive here in dependence on others. Whether we like it or not, there is hardly a moment of our lives when we do not benefit from others' activities. For this reason, it is hardly surprising that most of our happiness arises in the context of our relationship with others.'

His Holiness the Dalai Lama, *Ethics for the New Millennium*

If the axiom 'it's not what you know, it's who you know' has any validity then part of personal development is having a network. Which is just a fancy way of saying that you know a lot of people and they know you. Of course 'you get by with a little help from your friends' but you'll get by even better if you have friends *and* a network.

In my corporate career I have found that when faced with a problem senior executives don't ask 'How do I solve this?' but 'Who do I know who has solved this?' and, coming a close second, 'Who do I know who can help me solve this?' After all, why would anybody want to reinvent the wheel?

Enjoying a large network of people is very useful and has been around for a long time, even before the 'old boys club', which some join whilst at Eton or Harrow, consolidate at Oxford or Cambridge and achieve full membership on joining the Guards or going into the City.

There is a misconception that 'networking' is somehow a dirty word: that it implies manipulation and using people for your own ends. On the other hand, some people are somewhat shy in asking for help or advice. If you are one of these people just reverse it and ask yourself, 'Would I be happy to do it for them if I was asked?'

Thus a network only works if its members are supportive of each other, giving as much as they take. And in reality most people actively enjoy being asked for help. It's good for the ego to feel that your knowledge is valuable to someone else.

Networking takes time and much effort but the rewards are great:

- It can open up new opportunities.
- It can help you to solve problems.
- It can help you to think in new ways.
- It can give you the opportunity to help someone else achieve something.
- It can keep you abreast of the latest news and developments in your field.
- It can provide a place to try out new ideas.

Networking really works. How would:

- Steve Jobs have done so well without Steve Wozniak's technical ability?
- Twitter ever come to fruition for the founders, Evan Williams and Biz Stone, without Jack Dorsey's help?
- Bill Gates have made it without friend and mentor Paul Allen?
- Pierre Omidyar's eBay have sold anything without Jeffrey Skoll?

So how to begin?

Regard every new person you meet as someone who might be able to help you in the future by becoming part of your network and you theirs; make it a reciprocal relationship towards your ambitions. While networking may take lots of time and effort the rewards are great, certainly in time saved, money and increased opportunity.

Networking is a two-way street so it also requires development of a personal philosophy – whenever you can, be a giver:

It's in the nature of networking that if you give to others as much as you can it will be returned. It's not a conditional 'give' as in the Godfather of Mafia fame; give unconditionally expecting

 'Cast thy bread upon the waters: for thou shalt find it after many days.'

Ecclesiastes 11:1

nothing back and then through your reputation as a giver somehow your network just grows.

How to start building your network

List everyone you know, yes absolutely everyone, from the categories below:

- family
- friends from school
- friends from college
- current activities
- alumni meetings
- work
- previous jobs
- current job(s)
- clients
- suppliers
- professional societies or clubs
- armed services
- church or voluntary work
- neighbours
- tailor, hairdresser, mechanic, etc.
- professionals (e.g. dentist, lawyer, etc.).

Think through how you might contact or socialise with these people and what you could offer or what assistance you might give. Remember networking is about give and take so work out what benefits you might bring to your prospective contacts.

Once you get going you'll be amazed. When a friend of mine started, he carried a network card in his pocket and every time a name popped into his head he wrote it down. He was so surprised when he recalled 250 people easily. A Christmas card list is another good starting point and, if possible, use your parents' and your partner's lists as well.

brilliant tips

Here are some hints to help you:

- Ask the people that you currently know for referrals in your areas of interest.

- Accept as many invitations as possible where you can make contact with people.

- Explore any opportunities to join formal networks – Rotary, Lions, business groups, etc.

- First impressions are often misleading so make an effort to know the person.

- Make yourself available to help others in their work and leisure projects.

- Always thank those who help you, especially those that give you referrals or recommend you.

- Develop a different leisure activity on a semi-regular basis.

- Collect business cards and make notes about the person.

- Follow up people you know, informing or sending them information or articles of interest.

- When it's in your interest always share your information or intellectual property.

'It isn't just what you know, and it isn't who you know. It is actually who you know and who knows you.'

Bob Burg, author

'More business decisions occur over lunch than at any other time, yet no MBA courses are given on the subject.'

Peter Drucker, management guru

One of my favourite quotes is:

'A poor person should take a rich person out to lunch.'

Anon

This might sound strange at first but just think of the advantages that would accrue to you of taking Richard Branson out for lunch. Let's make it a posh lunch at Alain Ducasse's place at The Dorchester in Park Lane. It might set you back £300 for the two of you but what would you get for your money?

● You could tap into his network (on the internet he has 2,750,000 hits so he must know a lot of people).

● Running the Virgin group of about 400 different companies his management advice on most subjects would be worth its weight in gold.

● You could contact almost anybody in Europe, America and the Asia Pacific region with the opening words – 'Sir Richard Branson suggested that I contact you since you …'

● You could dine out on the event for years to come – 'When I last had lunch with Sir Richard Branson we chatted about …' That would impress anyone from board table to dinner table, from prince to pauper and all that for 300 quid!

I would not be surprised if, in the future, another company was born called 'Virgin Lunch'. Once a month Sir Richard would welcome you to lunch with himself and seven other participants for £250 a head. That works out at about £1000 per hour – not bad because the overheads are minimal and Sir Richard has to eat at midday anyway! However, I digress, so let's get back to networking.

How to introduce yourself: The Big Three

Obviously it's wise to make your first meeting with a prospective network colleague as easy and comfortable as possible for the two of you. Here are the first three questions we usually ask of someone when we meet them for the first time whether it's at a friend's party, when you are on holiday or attending a conference:

1 What is your name?

2 Where do you live?

3 What do you do?

Now I am not going to get very far with my potential new person if I just reply: 'Max, Bondi Beach, Psychologist.' Here I might get a response such as 'How interesting' as the person looks over my shoulder to see if they can move on quickly to someone more interesting.

When meeting someone for the first time we have to help them make conversation and we can do this very simply by offering more information. Giving information about yourself encourages the other person to do the same and before you can say 'network' you are deep in conversation and beginning a possible friendship or making a fresh contact.

So recommendations for the three questions are to add:

1 self-disclosure as to where you fit in

2 a tourist tip about where you live

3 a short résumé about what you do.

For example:

1 'Max – I am a friend of ...', or 'I wanted to be here because ...', or 'I have been in Australia for 16 years', etc.

2 'Bondi Beach – the haven of backpackers, beef burgers and beach beauties.'

3 'I'm a psychologist – I help organisations make sensible people decisions. I suppose I am an organisational astrologer' or 'I predict how people will react to various management options. In this way management decisions have a people input besides just the financial implications.'

You might think, well that's easy if you are a professional and so have something interesting to say, but the formula works in any situation. When I first left home, if I'd known this stuff, my network would have grown more quickly if I had said:

1 'Max – you can tell by my accent I've not been here long.'

2 'Plaistow – where there are 19 pubs and a church known as St Andrew's by the Sewer.'

3 'Wine stacker – I'm the chap that stacks about 1000 bottles of French wine a day so that you can enjoy it five years later. There's lots to know about wine and you have to be careful not to be ripped off.'

Now if I meet someone for the first time and they cannot respond to any of these introductory statements then I don't think that I would want them in my network anyway.

If you go to an event to meet people, lots of people will be employing similar networking techniques. Give yourself an edge similar to mine – who could possibly forget someone who stacks

u thousand bottles of French wine a day? However, make it even easier for the other person by having some business cards professionally made for yourself, if your organisation does not provide them, and especially if you are looking for employment. So you now have a new hobby and, if you are unemployed, a part-time job: that of 'business card collector.'

But what do I ask after the two of us have exhausted the big three above? Here are some obvious suggestions:

At business functions:

● How are things in your market just now?

● What is the best thing about your business (or job?)

● What is the latest fashion in your business – we have only just caught up with 'integrated team dynamics'?

● Who is your biggest competitor?

● How are you separating yourselves from the competition?

At social meetings

● How far away is that from your work?

● What is the schooling like in your area?

● What restaurant would you recommend in your area?

● What do you do for leisure besides PTA meetings like this?

● What did you do for your holiday this (or last) year?

Notice here that all the questions are what are known as 'open questions', questions which, unless you are a teenager, cannot be answered with a short two-word phrase or the shorter 'Yes' or 'No'.

Depending on the situation,[1] make sure that you have your own conversational, amusing if possible, answers to the big three just

---

1 I once had a friend who asked a very senior churchman what he did during the week. My friend's network did not progress.

in case it gets reciprocal, or someone else has also invested in this brilliant book!

 example

The great storm

On 16 October 1987 a great storm, with winds gusting up to 70 knots (130 km or 81 mph), struck Southern England. Everyone was affected and everyone had a story to tell so for at least two years after at social events there was the predictable question, 'How were you affected by the storm?' You would not have to say anything for the next 20 minutes! It was said that God sent the storm so that stiff-upper-lipped Englishmen could talk to each other when they first met.

A system for remembering

Psychologists tell us that we can 'know' about 250 people and after that it becomes very difficult, so it's important to develop a system regarding who you have met and if they are suitable to be in the reciprocal helping club. As soon as you can after meeting them, write down some notes about the person, where you met and the date, etc. It's important to do this because when you ring them in 18 months wanting to know the best way to tie a Bead Head Aggravator or Hare's Ear for a six or eight hook you can say: 'You will remember that we met at the Flanagans' house party and talked about fly fishing.'

They are going to be so flattered that:

● you remembered them
● they have an expertise that you don't
● you kept their card, and
● you sent them a clipping from *Time* magazine about the best fly fishing rivers in the world about three months ago.

Another useful gambit is to remember something personal about the person even if it's just as simple as whether they take sugar in their coffee or a twist in their G&T. Better still, try to remember something unique. When someone meets me again how special do you think it feels when they say, 'I'm doing my best to drink your thousand bottles of French wine but I remember that you are a chardonnay man' or 'How are those Jack Russell's of yours, Max? Still giving you an excuse to walk to see the beach?'

The dentist story

This will stretch your credibility but it's a true story. As you know, dentists do their best to relieve your nerves before they start on the drill work. From his repertoire of initial questions, the dentist asked his nervous patient, 'So what do you do?', and the patient replied 'I'm a production engineer but unfortunately I have just been made redundant.' 'No! Really?', came the dentist's reply, 'My last patient was from Laser Engineering and he was complaining that he just couldn't get a good production engineer! I'll give him a call if you like – give me your number.' Strange but true, so list everyone you know – including your dentist – and especially if you're a production engineer!

How to network at conferences, business presentations and social gatherings

- First, do not make a beeline for the buffet and the booze since it's difficult to shake hands and give and receive business cards with both hands full let alone being able to talk with your mouth full.

- Second, when you reach the door to the event, pause to survey the room. Who looks interesting, who looks popular, who is amusing a group? Those are the people that you want to meet.

- Third, do not drift to one of the walls for protection, or worse, hide in the corner. From the wall position, you can only be seen by the people in front of you. Having a wall behind you is for heroes in Hollywood action movies but in networking it's good to have someone socially 'attack' you from behind. Whenever and wherever possible stay centred.

- Fourth, if you can't break into a group, form your own group by approaching someone on their own. Like you, they don't want to be seen as if they have something contagious. If there is a 'single' nearby, invite them into the group, introduce your new colleague and give them an update on your discussion, then ask them for their opinion. Soon you will have people drifting over to your group and people will want your card because you know people.

Social leaders usually scan the room to see who they should be talking to. If you are in the 'scan' catch the person's eye and give a friendly nod as if you known them from way back. Then later you can just join their group with the same nod or smile or introduce yourself to the group, making sure that you 'sweep' the whole group.

Most of us go on seminars and attend conferences. Here, if you can, try and get a copy of the attendance list so that you can select who you would like to meet and how they spell and pro-nounce their name.

At the breaks, circulate as much as possible giving your cards out like confetti. Collect them, too, as if they were petrol vouchers. Wear your name tag – yes we all hate it and why would you put a pinhole in your expensive business clothes in the first place? Because most of us can remember faces but not names. If, like me, you find it difficult to speak to someone that you don't know, the tag at least puts a crack in this interpersonal ice as you use their name before you ask the 'big three' questions above.

The opportunities for networking are vast. Growing larger and larger by the minute are the internet network organisations such as LinkedIn, and Facebook with over 35 million participants. If Facebook were a country it would be the third largest in the world. Nor must we forget those business and professional networking organisations springing up like mushrooms on a warm summer's night. If there isn't one that fits 'you' why not develop one yourself?

Becoming a network star

Just as a star gives light, so in your networking give as much light as you can to others. Networking is not just about looking after and advancing self, it's being reciprocal, even pre-emptive, in your support. If you expect to receive, then you must expect to give. It is a privilege to support others in their needs and what is strange is that the more you support others the more you support yourself and the more you are supported.

Supporting others, providing information, sharing your experience, offering advice (if wanted) proactively – all will ensure that you expand the boundaries of your network. Soon you will develop a reputation as a source of information and someone who always knows useful or influential people.

brilliant tips

For meetings, seminars and conferences

- Most people take up networking opportunities to gain business. Big mistake: no one buys or does a deal on a first meeting. Most people also act like guests or attendees at such events. So be different. You are just there to meet people – act as if it were your event and you are the host.

- Arrive early, find out the location of the food, drinks, wastepaper baskets (to dispose of turned up sandwiches and well matured cocktail sausages), cloakrooms, etc. Look down the name cards or guest list so you have an idea of who is who and then be the host. Smile, welcome, directly introduce and work the room. You will find that people will gravitate towards you even if it's just to ask where the toilet is. Later you can go up to them and, introducing yourself, say 'Did you find it?', and then off you go with the big three initial questions.

- Once your network grows you will know people 'who know people' so then you can gain a reputation for putting people together where there is a mutual or shared interest. Again this will provide more contacts as new people will contact you to see if 'you know someone who ...'

- Network stars also send handwritten thank you notes when they are given support in any area. In the corporate world even Christmas cards are printed so you can imagine the impact your handwritten, yes handwritten, note will have. How long does it take to write

  'Great to meet (or catch up with) you last night at Flanagan's and I just wanted to say thank you so much for recommending that book, *Brilliant Personal Development*. I'm looking forward to telling you how much my team have come on as a result ...

  All the best'

And, of course, use a handwritten envelope and a real stamp: you are being personal, not corporate, and ensuring a network connection.

brilliant recap

- The advantages of networking are personified by the success of Apple, Microsoft, eBay and Twitter.

- When building your network, list out everyone you know by sourcing from Christmas card lists, etc.

- Introducing yourself involves some self-disclosure, a tourist tip and a short résumé.

- Make sure you ask open questions to keep things going.

- To become a network star: don't try to sell; discover what's what; discover who's who; act the host; write thank you notes; and follow up.

Final words

While you are thinking about yourself and your life, here are some concluding thoughts for you.

Do not take anything personally

This is the best way to obtain control over whatever life throws at you – good or bad. Life is just the way it is, not because you deserve it, or because you are better than anyone else or even because you are lucky. Similarly when bad things happen for which you are not responsible, that's just the way it is. You are not bad, your parents and ancestors were not bad either. When you don't take things personally you remain in control and forgiveness comes easily. If you don't forgive, the hurt and the damage done will be like a canker and will always stay with you.

 'It's not that I'm so smart, it's just that I stay with problems longer.'

Albert Einstein

Skills covered in this text, and any other skills for that matter, take practice. Practice cannot be delegated.

Nikos Kazantzakis (author of *Zorba the Greek*) once said:

'Ideal teachers are those who use themselves as bridges over which they invite their students to cross, then having facilitated their

crossing, joyfully collapse, encouraging them to create bridges of their own.'

I sincerely hope that this text will continue to be helpful in your future. Please read my final, unoriginal yet incredibly powerful, piece of advice to live by:

 '"Just do it"[1]
And do it brilliantly.
Omnia mutantur nos et mutamur in illis.'

Literally: 'All things change and we change with them.'

Max-Augustine +

Community Priest
The Communities of Our Lady
Sydney, Australia

---

1 Nike's 1988 advertising campaign slogan

Index

purging 192–8, 205
positive 198, 205
Vroom, Victor 139

weaknesses 43–4, 105
wealth xxii, 27, 55, 78–9, 130–1,
    225
White, Jesse 122
Wilde, Oscar 167
Williams, Evan 295
Wisconsin, University of xxv

withdrawing 145
work xv, 57, 82, 94–5, 252, 296,
    299–300, 304–5
worst case scenario 258
Wozniak, Steve 295
writing things down 107, 155

yoga and tai chi 261

Zen philosophy 63, 210, 261